Overcoming Ageism

Women *at* Work
Inspiring conversations, advancing together

The **HBR WOMEN AT WORK SERIES** spotlights the real challenges and opportunities women experience throughout their careers. With interviews from the popular podcast of the same name and related articles, stories, and research, these books provide inspiration and advice for taking on topics at work like inequity, advancement, and building community. Featuring detailed discussion guides, this series will help you spark important conversations about where we're at and how to move forward.

Books in the series include:

Making Real Connections

Next-Level Negotiating

Overcoming Ageism

Speak Up, Speak Out

Taking Charge of Your Career

Thriving in a Male-Dominated Workplace

You, the Leader

Women *at* Work

Inspiring conversations, advancing together

Overcoming Ageism

Harvard Business Review Press
Boston, Massachusetts

The web addresses referenced in this book were live and correct at the time of the book's publication but may be subject to change.

Cataloging-in-Publication data is forthcoming.

ISBN: 978-1-64782-581-2
eISBN: 978-1-64782-582-9

The paper used in this publication meets the requirements of the American National Standard for Permanence of Paper for Publications and Documents in Libraries and Archives Z39.48-1992.

CONTENTS

Contents

SECTION FOUR

Nurture Relationships and Create Support Systems

SECTION FIVE

Navigating Challenging Situations

Contents

SECTION SIX

It's Time to Fix the System

INTRODUCTION

It's Never the Right Age to Be a Woman

by Amy Bernstein, cohost of *Women at Work*

The hardest thing about sitting down to write the introduction to a book about ageism is admitting to yourself that you're subject to it.

I spent much of my early career as the "kid" at the table. Being one of the younger people in any work conversation was sometimes heady, but more frequently it was intimidating—especially when I felt ignored by my more seasoned colleagues. Now, on our *Women at Work* podcast, I frequently weigh in as the voice of experience, offering my perspective based on 40 years in the business. I'm lucky, though; despite those early slights, I've mostly sidestepped the injustices and insults that many women contend with both when they first enter the workforce and as they age past 50.

The World Health Organization defines ageism as "the stereotypes (how we think), prejudice (how we feel) and discrimination (how we act) towards others or oneself based on age," and it is rampant. A 2022 survey by the AARP found that 90 percent of respondents age 50 or older had experienced some form of age discrimination, ranging from hearing negative comments to being denied a job or promotion.[1] To be sure, in the United States and many other places, refusing to hire someone because of their age is illegal, but subtler forms of ageism—devaluing contributions from older employees, failing to consider them for plum gigs—is not. It will surprise no one reading this that the AARP also found that women feel the effects, including depression and financial insecurity, more than men do, with women of color feeling them most acutely.[2]

As I learned early on, older workers aren't the only ones facing age discrimination. It's a problem for younger employees as well. Section 1 of this collection—"Ageism Cuts Both Ways"—lays out the facts and debunks common assumptions. In chapter 2, HBR associate editor Emma Waldman shares her own experience and points to a 2019 study from Glassdoor that found that younger employees are *more* likely than older employees to have witnessed or experienced ageism at work. Maybe it's snarky comments about Gen Z or being called diminutive pet names. Maybe it's being left out of important decisions or meetings. Maybe it's not being given opportunities to take on important tasks because your abilities are questioned. As Waldman says, "Reverse ageism is real."

It's not enough to recognize ageism when you see it. You need to be able to navigate and address the problem while moving forward in your career. This book offers advice to women of all ages in doing just that, focusing on a few key areas.

In section 2 of this collection, we advise you to "build credibility and advocate for yourself." Who doesn't relate to executive coach Dorie Clark's point in chapter 4: "We all hope our merits will be recognized—and it's jarring when they're not. Some people begin to doubt themselves. Others get angry at the people who have failed to see their potential (or their actual demonstrated ability)." (I have feet in both camps.) Her sage advice? "The best plan is to ensure we're vigilant up front about conveying our expertise—and that if we falter in an encounter, we move quickly to correct those misimpressions." You must make sure that you are your best advocate and make it clear what you're bringing to your team and your organization.

You also need to make sure that you stay current with new thinking, new technology, and new approaches. As we advise in section 3, you must "keep developing, keep growing"—and this goes for older and younger women alike. For younger people, it's about proving that they're open to learning as they advance their career. For more experienced or senior workers, it's about showing that they can admit that they don't know everything but are open—and interested in—continuing to expand their knowledge and skills.

It also helps to "nurture relationships and create support systems," as section 4 recommends. One vital point: Make sure your network includes people of all ages. In "Mentorship Goes Both Ways," consultant Cynthia J. Young argues that when networks include older and younger people, "junior employees gain more access to social networks and build their leadership skills. Senior employees gain a fresh perspective and expand their knowledge around new trends or technologies. Everyone becomes more engaged." Goodness knows, I'd be nowhere without the generous mentorship I got from more senior editors—people whom I admired for their integrity and openness as much as for their skills with the blue pencil. In turn, I continue to learn so much from my less experienced colleagues, who see the world so differently from the way I do.

While these three sections offer general advice on how to triumph in the face of ageism, we know there are instances that would test even the most dauntless among us. In section 5, we offer help in "navigating challenging situations." Menopause, for example, with its hot flashes, brain fog, and other attendant discomforts. Alicia A. Grandey of Penn State has advice for dealing with the stigma and, perhaps more important, for normalizing a perfectly *normal* phase of life. For more junior women who aren't sure when to push back, HBR senior editor Paige Cohen gives smart advice on how to decline low-priority work, even if the request comes from your boss. (Their insights are pretty useful for those of us who are still dealing with this problem even after decades of experience.) And Jodi Glickman, CEO of leadership development firm Great on the Job, offers tips for what to do when you're younger than the people you manage.

Finally, we can't leave the work of addressing the problem of age discrimination to individual initiative, relationships, luck, or even the law. Like any form of bias, ageism is often woven into the workplace culture, and like any form of bias, we must deal with it transparently and decisively on a broad scale. Indeed, as section 6 declares, "It's time to fix the system." To that end, professors Amy Diehl, Leanne M. Dzubinski, and Amber L. Stephenson offer concrete ideas in "How Organizations Can Recognize—and End—Gendered Ageism." Their four-part remedy: recognize age bias, address "lookism" (don't get me started on this), focus on skills—no matter who has them—and cultivate creative collaborations.

One clear theme throughout this collection is that we can't battle age bias without help. Nor should we. We need our colleagues, our friends, our allies, and our leaders. We need each other. I hope that by understanding how ageism works, how it affects us all, and how to address it, we are better equipped to fight it, so that someday none of us will feel the sting of being devalued because of our age.

Ageism Cuts Both Ways

1

Aging Up, Not Out

A conversation with Nancy Morrow-Howell

Ageism is just one of the biases women face in the workplace. Whether you're too old or too young, you're not taken seriously, your ideas are shot down, and you miss vital opportunities to advance your career.

Nancy Morrow-Howell is a social policy professor at Washington University in St. Louis, Missouri, and she directs the University's Friedman Center for Aging. In this conversation, *Women at Work* cohosts Amy Bernstein and Amy Gallo talk to Nancy about how older women are treated in the workplace, the feelings of invisibility as they age in their careers, and the resilience that comes with experience.

AMY GALLO: Since you've identified as an older adult, have you noticed that people treat you differently?

NANCY MORROW-HOWELL: Yes. I'm in a very privileged position, being a faculty member with an endowed professorship at Wash U, so I can't complain about much. But even in that privileged environment, I feel like people treat older adults differently. We are still very ageist, and I have become more aware of that, mainly because I'm studying it more. There's the concept of implicit bias—that we're not even aware of how ageist we are when we interact with people or think about our organizations.

I hear plenty of older people say that they sense that they are viewed as more irrelevant. They say "invisible," but I think *irrelevant* is a better word. Age discrimination is illegal on paper, but older adults are still often treated differently in terms of opportunities and leadership positions offered, and just have a sense of being overlooked for new engagements, especially when looking for a job.

AMY BERNSTEIN: I'd love to pass along a question from one of our listeners. Christina writes: "We are a cohort of 50- to 60-year-old women who are productive, capable, experienced with wisdom and the ability to see context. In the workforce, because of our age and our gray hairs, we are seen as not technically capable," which she says is not true. They're seen as "not forward thinking" and "perhaps too experienced and expensive and, after a workforce reduction, not candidates to hire." She asks, "Are these anecdotal observations valid? Are they validated by research?"

NANCY: She is right that those are the common perceptions. But most of them can be invalidated through research.

Looking at her perception that women are more expensive—because people have been on a job a long time (there are cost-of-living increases, and time generally leads to raises)—older workers' salaries can be higher than others. But the cost of training people and replacing people who aren't as committed to a job is greater than those costs. And in fact, despite older adults having higher risks for different chronic conditions, there is less absenteeism among them.

So a lot of those things we can confront with the facts. Older workers just have to keep it up. They have to work on self-development. They have to work on staying digitally competent. There's no resting on any laurels, and that takes energy. People of any age need to do it, but older workers are accused of not having as much energy. We need to make sure that we're demonstrating that, yeah, we do.

AMY G.: How have you been doing that yourself?

NANCY: By what I'm doing right now, being interviewed by you all. On older workers' CVs, it's always a challenge. They can't be, "Here's 20 pages and all my experience." Who cares? It has to be short and well-framed. And there are new sections of CVs, like your social media, right? Your different opportunities—maybe a podcast, blog, or media coverage. I need to pay more attention to that kind of stuff in my CV or on my webpage because it's not something that I'm used to.

AMY G.: How do you stay on top of what is happening and what needs to be done?

NANCY: Well, I haven't 100%, because it really is hard. I'm just lucky because I'm in an environment surrounded by young people. I have good relationships with my kids and grandkids, so I just try to be exposed and not say, "Oh, I don't like that stuff." I try to figure out what it is.

That's a good example of sort of the energy it takes. You have to be proactive. That's why some people do eventually want to step back and retire and say, "Oh, I don't want to put in that energy anymore, I'm ready to do something different."

AMY B.: A lot of women feel that they kind of disappear as they get older in the workplace. What are your thoughts on that?

NANCY: I have that sense from colleagues whom I talk to, and a bit of my own experience. There's a feeling of being overlooked as people turn to folks who are a little younger. For me, when people ask me, "When are you going to retire?" I think, "Hmm, I'm thinking about it, but are they asking me because they think I *should*? Are they are giving me a hint?" But it's a very common question to older people. That carries a lot of emotional messages, too, where you begin to question yourself, your relevance, or your competency. So that's one way that I see it.

AMY B.: Say you're in a meeting, and the group turns to the younger person at the table. How do you handle that if you're an older woman and feel that you have something to contribute on the subject at hand?

NANCY: For myself, I just have to know that I do have something to contribute, and not accept the situation as being overlooked unless it's warranted. I mean, I want my younger colleagues to take leadership. More power to them. I want to help them do it. I just don't want the experienced and the more mature worker's voice to be excluded for ageist reasons.

AMY B.: So you would advise asserting yourself appropriately?

NANCY: Yeah, assert yourself appropriately and have good things to contribute. I do think there's also a kind of slippery slope. Don't say, "Well, when we did this then . . ." and, "Forty years ago . . ." Don't drag up the old history lesson when you're presenting an idea. But I do feel so often I can frame something in a historical perspective. Like, "We tried that a handful of years ago and this is what worked and this is what didn't." Just be careful that you're not the one who always starts with a long story from "how we used to do it."

AMY G.: I want to go back to what you said about people asking you about when you're going to retire. How do you respond to that question?

NANCY: Very honestly, because I have been thinking about it. I've always said that I would work until I'm 70, and then I'd start some sort of a step-down plan. So I tell people that. All the colleagues around me are thinking about it and talking about it, and I don't think people are trying to be mean or imply that I should be retiring. I think they're generally curious because it's such a normal thing that's expected of people in their mid-sixties. But it's certainly changing.

Next time, I think I'm going tell them my plan, then say, "I'm wondering why you asked that? What are you thinking? Or what are you thinking about me?" I'd like to see if I can discover what people are thinking when they ask me that question.

AMY G.: It might force them to reflect on why, right? Because this is often implicit bias. It might encourage them to reflect on what caused them to ask that question.

NANCY: Yeah.

AMY B.: If you sense, as an older woman in the workforce, that you're not getting the same kind of professional development opportunities as your younger colleagues, how do you bring that up with your boss or with HR?

NANCY: I don't know about you all, but we have annual reviews that include our self-perceptions and our desires for what we need to improve and how we might do it. I would make sure that I had a very well-developed and articulated plan for myself for professional development that includes real concrete things that I could do to say, *Here's what I need and here's how I can get it done.* Don't leave it to anybody's imagination.

AMY G.: Much of the implicit bias toward older workers can often be confused with empathy. You're thinking, *Well, this person must want to spend time with their grandchildren*, or *They must be tired.* One tactic might be to just look at your thinking when those protectionist attitudes come into play. Are you really doing right by your older workers if you're just so concerned about them?

NANCY: I love that point. We're very paternalistic. In fact, there's a thing called *compassionate ageism*: "I need to protect, to relieve, to take care of and support, because most people think all older adults need help."

A question we can always ask ourselves and our employees is, "What does age have to do with this?" Generally, the answer is "not a lot," because we think age means some-one can't do something or they must not want to do some-thing. But individual motivation, preference, capability, function—those things are not necessarily about age.

AMY G.: We've talked a lot about the challenges. What are the benefits for older workers, especially people who are working past age 65, for example?

NANCY: Oh, there are so many. Number one, we have to work longer because we don't have the savings that we need to live so long after we stop working. So there's pressure to keep working because we have to—but also because we want to. We know that working in general produces health for people. Cognitive health, social health, physical health—those things are good. Now that's not true for all workers. It depends on your job. Being in real heavy-duty, physical work isn't necessarily good. But when people have the social connections and the cognitive engagement, we can certainly show that that helps people maintain and improve their health.

AMY B.: Are there benefits in having all that experience from having been around the block or sort of knowing how things go that accrue as you get older?

NANCY: Yes. That maturity allows people to have a different perspective, more of a long-run perspective where they can find the positive and withstand the negative a little bit more since they've been around the block.

AMY B.: You might say that older women in the workforce are more resilient.

NANCY: I think so. They are by definition. They've been around the block and are still there. There's a certain resiliency or survivorship to these folks. Then there are also the experiences that taught people how to roll with the punches a little bit more.

Adapted from "Aging Up, Not Out" on Women at Work *(podcast), season 4, episode 8, December 2, 2019.*

2

Am I Old Enough to Be Taken Seriously?

by Emma Waldman

started my career in New York City, working as an editorial assistant for one of the largest publishing conglomerates in the world. Fresh out of grad school, with several years of internship experience in tow, I walked into the 52-story building with my head held high. I was to report directly to the senior vice president, an industry legend. She was poised and intelligent, and I idolized her.

During my second week on the job, I received her email invitation for an in-person meeting. Heart racing, I dashed through the doors of her corner office, which overlooked Broadway and West 56th. Expecting to receive my first real assignment, she looked at me and said, "Emma, I just received a package from IKEA. Would you mind assembling my new lamp? Let me know when you're finished."

I would love to dismiss this humiliating—yet humbling—moment as one bad thing that happened a very long time ago. But it still triggers me today: a woman approaching 30 with seven years of job experience under my belt. As one of the youngest people on my team by a decade, I'm often hesitant to assert myself in meetings or ask more seasoned colleagues for help out of fear of seeming naive. In these moments, I find myself back in the corner office, building my first boss's IKEA lamp and trying to figure out her intentions. Was it because I seemed incompetent? Was it because my role included "assistant" in the title?

Or was it what I feared then—and still fear now—that my age makes it hard for others to take me seriously? Was I, in fact, experiencing ageism? (See the box, "What Ageism Is.")

I needed to figure out if this insecurity has grounds in reality. Here's what the research tells me: When you Google "age discrimination at work," you'll find article after article about bias against older employees and laws aimed at addressing this problem. In the United States, the federal government has protections in place to prevent discrimination against workers age 40 and up. Companies can't, for example, legally assume that someone isn't qualified for a job because they are "too old" to understand how to use a certain technology or implement the latest innovations. That said, it's questionable whether these protections always work. Ageism against

What Ageism Is

BY NICOLE D. SMITH

At its core, ageism is discrimination based on age. The World Health Organization (WHO) divides ageism into several layers: how we think (stereotypes), how we feel (prejudices), and how we act toward others or even ourselves (discrimination) because of age. Taken together, the WHO reports, those types of behaviors can affect physical and mental health and can even shorten people's lives by up to seven and a half years.

Researcher Justyna Stypińska and sociologist Konrad Turek conducted an extensive study that shows ageist behaviors at work can take two forms: *hard* and *soft*.[a] Hard age discrimination is illegal or prohibited behaviors, such as firing, demoting, or severely harassing someone because of age. Soft discrimination, like an off-color joke or comment, isn't necessarily illegal and occurs mostly in interpersonal interactions. The soft form is the more common one, and women experience it more often than men. Since soft discrimination is rooted mostly in stereotypes, it can lead to people not valuing coworkers' contributions and perspectives and even negatively assessing their skill sets.

The primary victims of ageist work cultures tend to be at the poles—the youngest and oldest workers.[b] Members of the first group are seen as inexperienced and having less to offer, which can make it difficult for them to find employment or negotiate with hiring managers for fair wages. Meanwhile, studies show that older people struggle to get promotions, find new work, and change careers; this is particularly true for women and underrepresented racial groups in the United States.[c] When ageism is rampant, older workers might be seen not only in a negative light but also as lower status than even very young peers, despite having lower turnover and high-rated job performance.[d]

In the workplace, ageism can be insidious and pervasive and can have a negative influence across groups. It can dissolve solidarity, limit the contributions of younger and older employees alike, and lead to people being devalued and excluded. Experts say that if managers allow ageist behaviors to persist, employee job satisfaction, engagement, and commitment all decline.

a. Justyna Stypińska and Konrad Turek, "Hard and Soft Age Discrimination: The Dual Nature of Workplace Discrimination," *European Journal of Ageing* 14 (2017): 49–61.
b. *Oxford Research Encyclopedia of Psychology*, s.v. "Ageism in the Workplace," by David M. Cadiz, Amy C. Pytlovany, and Donald M. Truxillo, March 29, 2017, https://doi.org/10.1093/acrefore/9780190236557.013.2.
c. Joo Yeoun Suh, "Age Discrimination in the Workplace Hurts Us All," *Nature Aging* 1 (2021): 147, https://doi.org/10.1038/s43587-020-00023-1.
d. Jamie L. Macdonald and Sheri R. Levy, "Ageism in the Workplace: The Role of Psychosocial Factors in Predicting Job Satisfaction, Commitment, and Engagement," *Journal of Social Issues* 72, no. 1 (2016): 169–190; "The 'Silver Tsunami': Why Older Workers Offer Better Value Than Younger Ones," *Knowledge at Wharton*, December 6, 2010, https://knowledge.wharton.upenn.edu/article/the-silver-tsunami-why-older-workers-offer-better-value-than-younger-ones/; Carlos A. Viviani

et al., "Productivity in Older Versus Younger Workers: A Systematic Literature Review," *Work* 68, no. 3 (January 2021): 577–618.

Adapted from "I Was a Manager in an Ageist Workplace" on hbr .org, March 8, 2022 (product #H06WHG).

older workers still runs rampant in some companies and industries.[1]

At the same time, these protections don't apply to young professionals. This is a problem. A recent study revealed that young adults are often more likely to report experiencing ageism at work than their middle-aged and older counterparts.[2] It's called *reverse ageism.*

On top of this, Glassdoor released a 2019 diversity and inclusion survey in the United States, United Kingdom, France, and Germany that found younger employees (52% of workers age 18 to 34) are more likely than older employees (39% of those age 55+) to have witnessed or experienced ageism at work.

"Ageism cuts both ways," Professor Dominic Abrams at the University of Kent told me. "It's true that people often apply patronizing stereotypes to older workers, and so they are often assumed to be less employable. But younger people tend to be more exposed to all forms of prejudice and discrimination than older people—racism, sexism, and ageism."

According to my research, this is what reverse ageism can look like: More senior or experienced employees overlooking feedback from younger colleagues on projects. Seasoned employees assuming that younger colleagues can't be trusted with important tasks. Or younger colleagues being the target of stereotypical age assumptions.

When I explore whether these examples fit into my own work experience, I'm brought back to one moment that took place before the Covid-19 pandemic got really bad in Boston. I was in the office, talking to a fellow 20-something-year-old coworker about an upcoming assignment. We were brainstorming ideas for a new product when a senior employee turned to us and said, "Girls, can you please take your chatter elsewhere? It's very distracting."

My peer and I exchanged a glance—confused and a little bit shocked. While our colleague may have thought he was just asking for quiet, there were assumptions embedded in his comment:

- **Assumption 1:** That we are "girls," not two grown women.

- **Assumption 2:** Our discussion was "chatter," as if we weren't working on anything of importance.

So no, not all of it is in my head.

I understand how it might be easy for people to mistrust those who have less workplace experience than themselves, but this mistrust ultimately works against all of us and can lead to biased assumptions. When older workers doubt the competency of those younger than them, they fail us. They are not helping the next generations develop transferable skills. They're building barriers of mistrust.

Will It Get Better?

Discrimination varies from person to person, and for this reason, organizations often struggle to tackle these biases on a wider scale. You can't force someone to think a certain way, but you can help them to better understand your position and perspective.

If you find yourself in a position like mine, here are few ideas I've started to put into practice to better my own situation. I hope they'll help you too:

Start or join a working group for young professionals

Keeping quiet about discrimination at work can be both mentally and emotionally draining—and can bleed into your life outside of the office over time. It's important to create a safe space to talk to people you trust about what you're going through. If your company doesn't already have a working group for young professionals, consider starting one yourself. This might take the form of a designated Slack channel in which you can talk openly and share experiences online. Or it might be a monthly Zoom call with a proposed agenda and discussion points. Either way, it will give people like yourself a place to talk about workplace concerns, find allies, and exchange ideas about how to remedy them.

Talk to your manager

Make your manager aware of the situation. They may have no idea what you're going through. During your next check-in, share your experiences and concerns. They might redirect you to an HR specialist who is trained in handling issues of discrimination at work, or help you devise a plan for confronting the perpetrator. If anything, your manager will know to keep their eyes peeled for future instances of ageism. Raising the issue is the first step toward combating it for good.

Alternatively, your manager might understand workplace discrimination all too well, and can serve as a role model and mentor in the future. One of my workplace mentors is a woman who has just as much professional experience as her male counterparts (if not more). Because we've both fallen victim to other workplace biases (in terms of gender discrimination) in the past, she was sympathetic toward my situation. She knew what it was like to feel undervalued because of something that's out of her control and offered me some actionable suggestions for overcoming these biases in the future.

Have an open discussion with the culprit

There's nothing wrong with respectfully approaching the coworker who is demonstrating discrimination against you to have an open dialogue. Sending an email that begins with, "The comment that you made during Tuesday's meeting made me feel uncomfortable. When you bring my age into a conversation, it sounds like you're assuming that I'm not qualified to do my job," is a great place to start. This could evolve into a larger conversation about ageism and how to overcome biases that might be clouding their judgment. If you feel comfortable, you could suggest working on a project together to build trust and demonstrate your expertise. You might even end up learning more about where this person's bias is coming from.

You might find, for example, that the culprit's behavior stems from an insecurity about their own performance and has nothing to do with you personally (though this is still not an excuse for their behavior).

Never forget your value add

When you're put down by someone at work, it can be easy to forget your value. But I can reassure you: You offer a special skill set and a unique perspective, which is why you were hired. Figure out what your "specialty" is—whether it's social media proficiency, communication skills, expertise with video or audio platforms, etc.—and use it to your advantage.

When the opportunity presents itself, remind your co-workers of what you bring to the table. You have insights and experiences that others do not. During meetings, chime in with ideas that highlight your skills and viewpoint. Take a quick pause and a deep breath to center yourself. You might say something like, "This could be a great opportunity to introduce a podcast," or, "As a Millennial, I can speak to the fact that many of our younger readers are looking for content on early career financial planning." Use your position to your advantage.

Most importantly, let these experiences inform your growth as you advance in your career. Don't let the fear that you'll never be taken seriously stay with you until you're old enough to be considered "seasoned." Set an example by trusting and asserting that young professionals know what they're doing, and work to become the kind of employee you'd want to work with, years down the line, when a young worker approaches you for help.

Adapted from content posted on Ascend, hbr.org, November 25, 2020.

3

Is That Conflict with Your Colleague Really About Age Difference?

by Amy Gallo

You've noticed a frustrating pattern. During meetings with an older colleague, they seem to tune out any time you offer an idea. You suspect they're checking email when you're speaking, and they rarely, if ever, acknowledge your suggestions. Given dismissive comments they've made about other employees around your age, you assume they're not taking you seriously because you're younger than they are.

Or perhaps the situation is reversed: You've caught a younger colleague rolling their eyes on group Zoom calls—seemingly whenever you're sharing experience with the topic at hand. The gesture could be aimed at someone else, but you can't help feeling that the colleague sees you as stuck in your ways and is acting disrespectfully on purpose.

But how can you be sure that what's happening between you and your coworker is a generational conflict? And if it is, how should you address it?

With as many as five generations working side by side in organizations, it's easy to get caught up in generational conflicts and stereotypes:

- Boomers are out of touch and arrogant.

- Gen Xers are cynical and disengaged.

- Millennials are entitled.

- Gen Zers are narcissistic and don't want to work hard.

If these stereotypes were all true, little would get done in most companies. After all, who wants to work with people who have any of these attributes? But stereotypes don't have to be true to create conflicts. Believing these things anyway—assuming that a colleague from a particular generation is a certain way—can cause rifts with our coworkers.

There's another layer that adds to the potential strain. If we assume that our older or younger colleagues believe these things *about us*, we may be setting ourselves up for unpleasant clashes. Researchers call these *meta-stereotypes*, or "what we think others believe about us based on our age group."

Ultimately, there is little evidence that people of different generations behave markedly differently from each other at work or want markedly different things from their careers.[1] Research has found, for example, that 20-year-olds tend to behave like 20-year-olds, no matter what generation they're in. And while it's common for people to lament how things have changed as they get older and more senior in their careers, the belief that "kids these days" are worse than young people in the past is more of an illusion than a reality.[2]

What isn't an illusion is the tension that beliefs about other generations—both yours and your colleagues'—create in your interactions. You feel judged, they feel judged. So what do you do if you're stuck in a conflict that has been created or exacerbated by a colleague's unfair assumptions? There are a few tactics you can use to avoid knee-jerk responses and improve your working relationships.

Be Curious About Your Response— and Theirs

When something goes wrong at work—say, a young colleague misses a deadline, causing an important project to be delayed—we tell ourselves a story about what's occurring, why, and what will happen next. And these stories, laden with emotions and critiques, feel truthful to us, even when they may not be, because they're based on our brain's sometimes-flawed sensemaking attempts rather than on facts. In an effort to conserve resources, our brains make snap judgments about what's going on and how we should react. Scientists call it *premature cognitive commitment.*

Maybe you assume that your colleague didn't get their work done on time because they're a 20-something who doesn't take work as seriously as you do. Instead of sticking with that story, take a step back and ask yourself what else might be going on. Here are some questions you can start with:

- Is it possible that my interpretation is wrong?

- What assumptions have I made about my colleague or the situation?

- How have I possibly contributed to the problem between us?

- Other than this person's age or generation, what else could explain their behavior?

That last question is important because of a cognitive bias called *fundamental attribution error*—the inclination to observe another person's behavior and assume it has more to do with their personality than with their circumstances. That's why you might tell yourself the project delay was a result of your colleague's lack of commitment when it was actually because, unbeknownst to you, they were dealing with a family crisis or simply had too much on their plate. Interestingly, we do the *opposite* when it comes to ourselves: If you're running behind on a project, you probably focus on all the reasons for the delay, not on the idea that you're from a generation of uncommitted workers.

Be Aware of Common Tensions

It can be easy to blame a conflict on generational differences because some stereotypes have kernels of truth to them. Believing that Boomers are technologically savvy might be hard if your Boomer parents, for example, are not.

Rather than seeing any differences as flaws in the other person, it can help to acknowledge that tensions regularly come up between people from different generations.

Table 3-1 shows some common tensions that can lead to conflicts. On the left are attributes and values that are frequently (and stereotypically) assigned to younger generations, and on the right are ones often linked to older people.

Recognizing that these tensions exist can help to depersonalize a disagreement you and your colleague are having. And you can go a step further and embrace the fact that these are often positive, even productive, tensions to navigate. Rather than determining who's "right" and who's "wrong," accept that people see the world differently—and that's not only OK but likely helpful to the work you're trying to accomplish together. For

TABLE 3-1

Common attributes assigned to generations

Younger generations	Older generations
Efficient communication	Rich communication
High technology	Low technology
Progressive values	Traditional values
Feeling entitled to advancement	Earning advancement
Innovation	Status quo
Life outside work	Commitment to work
Egalitarian	Hierarchical
Focus on meaning	Focus on money

instance, if you're always pushing to try new things and an older colleague tends to argue that what has worked previously should be preserved, your team is more likely to land on a good balance between innovating and sticking with the tried-and-true.

Name the Bias and Commit to Challenging It

Putting a label on the dynamic between you and a co-worker can be tempting: "This might be an age thing . . ." or "We're from different generations, so. . . ." But statements like those can backfire, even if you intend them to be helpful or clarifying. People immediately feel defensive when you attribute their behaviors, especially one you're annoyed with, to their entire generation.

This doesn't mean you shouldn't talk about generational differences. Naming the tensions can be useful, but be careful not to pigeonhole your colleague. Instead, you might call out stereotypes. For example, you could say something along the lines of, "According to the media, my generation is lazy and yours is stuck in their ways. I think we can agree that neither of those things is true." Or "I know there are a lot of misconceptions about both of our generations—that people my age are out of touch and people your age are entitled. That's not how I see myself or you." You might even follow up with a promise: "If I have a problem or potential conflict, I won't attribute it to your age or generation. I'll address the issue directly, and I hope you'll do the same for me."

Emphasize Similarities, Not Differences

We are more likely to empathize with people if we identify with them in some way. Rather than emphasizing (even in your own mind) all the ways you're dissimilar from your colleague, find ways to show them you're alike. Ask a younger colleague what it's like to be starting out in your industry or what challenges they're excited about taking on. Ask an older colleague what it was like coming up in the industry or what kinds of obstacles they've had to overcome in their career. Then, listen and relate where you can, sharing your own experience. Expressing interest can disarm tension.

Seeking advice is another way to bridge a perceived gap. What does the other person have to teach you? What could you use their counsel on? You can say something like, "I know we often see things a bit differently, so I'd love to get your perspective on this."

Focus on a Shared Goal

Along the same lines, it can help to align yourself with your colleague. Is there a task or a project that you can tackle together, channeling your collective talents and energy in positive ways? Or a problem you can help them solve?

Teaming up with a coworker whom you feel is judging you may be unappealing. But having a shared goal could help ease the tension and get you pulling in the same direction. Here are some ways you could suggest this:

- "I know we both care about getting this project done on time. Can we talk about how we can work together to accomplish that?"

- "We can both make our team/department look good here."

- "I think we'd knock it out of the park if we took this on together."

Agree on How You'll Work Together

It goes without saying, but so many conflicts are the result of misalignment on how best to get things done. One way to address a current conflict, and prevent future ones, is to make clear how you and your colleague will work together. Just because you're on the same team and care about the same goal doesn't mean you'll have the same preferences. So take the time to have conversations about the processes you'll use to collaborate, and be willing to accommodate what your colleague wants. Flexibility is key. Maybe you believe text messages are the most efficient way to handle in-the-moment issues; your colleague may disagree. Or perhaps you prefer to send summary notes after your meetings, even though your coworker doesn't think they're necessary.

I've worked with people who write down their work preferences in a "user guide" to help jump-start those conversations. The document explains everything from why they're vegan (and how that might impact team meals) to their typical work hours to the value they place on efficiency. It wasn't a list of demands about how we would work together, but a way for us to align on exactly how we'd communicate, give feedback, and interact.

. . .

One thing I find helpful when working with people of various ages is reminding myself that age is just a point in time. It's cliché, I know, but we are all getting older. To cut through my instinct to stereotype or judge coworkers of other generations, I have a mantra: "That was me. That will be me." Whether I'm frustrated with a younger coworker who keeps coming up with new ways of doing things or annoyed with an older colleague who starts sentences with "When I was your age . . . ," I try to remind myself that I was once there, and I will likely be there. We all will.

Adapted from content on hbr.org, March 8, 2022 (product #H06W60).

Build Credibility and Advocate for Yourself

4

Convey Your Experience When Meeting Someone New

by Dorie Clark

We all hope our résumé and experiences will speak for themselves. But many of us are underestimated by the people we come into contact with, especially when those first impressions are based on our gender or age. With coworkers or others we see regularly, we can overcome negative perceptions through hard work and behavioral change. But how do you make a strong first impression on someone you're just meeting—and avoid falling into their unthinking mental frameworks?

I've certainly been there. A few years ago, I met a retired professor from a top business school. At the time, I had already taught at one business school and hoped to teach at more. I thought he might be able to offer advice about how to break in at his school. He waved me off dismissively. "*Every* executive wants to teach at our business school," he told me. "My best advice is to apply to the doctoral program, and maybe you could be a TA."

A year after that, I connected with an executive who ran a respected conference. I was thrilled when, at the end of our meeting, he introduced me to his employee who was in charge of recruiting speakers. "I wanted to introduce you two—you should follow up," he said. I assumed the intro from her boss would have paved the way for an invitation to present, but just minutes into our follow-up meeting, I realized she literally knew *nothing* about me and had no idea why I was there. Suddenly, I was thrust into an unexpected "Prove yourself" mode. At the end of the conversation, she turned to me: "I'm always looking for good speakers," she told me. "If you can think of anyone, let me know."

We all hope our merits will be recognized—and it's jarring when they're not. Some people begin to doubt themselves. Others get angry at the people who have failed to see their potential (or their actual demonstrated ability). But the best plan, of course, is to ensure we're vigilant up front about conveying our expertise—and that if we falter in an encounter, we move quickly to correct those misimpressions.

Before you meet a new contact, make sure they're aware of your background and expertise. I assumed the conference organizer had been fully briefed by her boss, but it was a costly mistake. She obviously could have been a lot more curious or organized, but setting the tone of the meeting was my responsibility, and I dropped the ball. Instead, as the famed psychologist Robert Cialdini advised when I interviewed him for my book *Reinventing You*, you should "send a letter of introduction that says, 'I'm looking forward to our interaction on Thursday on the topic of X, and my background and experience with regard to X are as follows.'" Says Cialdini, "It's perfectly appropriate to say those things in a letter of introduction, but it's not appropriate as soon as there's a face-to-face interaction because you look like a boastful braggart and a self-aggrandizer." The letter of introduction establishes your authority before you even step in the room, which would have helped me immeasurably.

During the meeting, have a number of anecdotes ready that demonstrate your expertise. You can likely predict the questions they'll ask; for each one, identify a story that showcases your abilities. For instance, if you're concerned someone might view you as "just another graduate student" seeking career advice, make sure you have stories ready that cite your professional experience to dispel their patronizing notions.

After the meeting, if you suspect they haven't fully grasped your potential, don't push it. I didn't argue with the business school professor that I was qualified to teach, or with the conference organizer that I was an excellent speaker. When it's clear someone has pigeonholed you, those protestations come off as slightly pathetic. Instead, recognize that you're in the long game now and you need to change their opinion of you over time. If the relationship is worth cultivating, keep in touch and periodically update them with news about your progress ("Just thinking of you, since I recently spoke at the XYZ conference"); if you have mutual friends, let them talk you up. They need to "discover you" and your value for themselves.

Meanwhile, don't let their limited judgment of you get you down. In the years following the dis from the retired business school professor, I've secured teaching engagements at four additional top business schools—I'm actually just back from guest lecturing at his own university.

. . .

Someday, if we're lucky, we may achieve enough recognition that our reputation always precedes us and people are always thrilled to do business with us. Until then, there will be people who don't have a clue what we can offer. To advance in our careers and get the respect we deserve, the only solution is to recognize it's our responsibility to ensure they find out.

Adapted from "Don't Let Them Underestimate You" on hbr.org, August 30, 2013 (product #H00B64).

5

Building a Personal Brand at Work—No Matter Your Age

by Nahia Orduña

Working hard has always kept me busy. As a college student, I took on two internships at once, only to find out neither company was hiring upon my graduation. In my first job at a big tech company, I went the extra mile to exceed my quarterly goals, only to be laid off three years in. Despite my efforts, my position was made redundant. A few years later, once I landed on my feet, I was assigned a major project by the head of my department at a telecommunications organization. Sadly, my boss was moved to another team, and the new leader completely dropped it.

In all these stories, I was so absorbed in my day-to-day tasks, so eager to meet expectations, that I had no time to think about my personal brand. Each time I changed roles or was forced to move on for factors outside of my control, I naturally thought, "I have to prove who I am and what I can do all over again."

What I wish I had known back then: If I had created a personal brand sooner, it would have saved me from constantly starting from scratch.

When most of us think of "personal brands," our minds wander to social media influencers singing, dancing, posing, or talking about fitness and fashion. These people are known for their expertise. They are up with the trends. They are trusted by their followers. Well, what if you had that same kind of influence at work? What if people in your field sought you out for advice and inspiration? Think of what that could do for your career.

The idea that employees should build their own personal brands has become popular in the past few years—and for good reason. To me, this means being up to date in your industry, making you more resilient and adaptable. It means being recognized for your unique self and skills and increasing your visibility, access to opportunities, and growth. A positive personal brand is beneficial to both you and your organization.

Given this, why don't more people develop one? In my experience, it's because we don't have the time. Building a personal brand is a real investment, and this can be tricky if you, like me, enjoy giving yourself fully to your job. It's even more difficult for young professionals, who may have less experience to build from. But even if you're older, you may find it hard to condense decades of work credentials into a cohesive brand.

So, how do you get started? The trick is to make your personal brand a fulfilling part of your day-to-day job. Here's how.

Define Your Personal Brand

When we work for corporations, it's easy to get sucked into the culture and blend our identities with that of our organizations. I've always been very proud of my employers. I enjoy wearing corporate colors and using the company jargon. If this is also the case for you, how do you develop a personal brand that lives within that larger corporate identity?

You need to identify three things:

- **Your uniqueness:** What unique perspective do you bring to the organization? Think about the vastness of your intersectional identity: your background, culture, race, ethnicity, gender identity, sexual orientation, class, caste, religious beliefs, and so on. Considering these factors, ask yourself: *How does my identity impact my understanding of the world and this business? What can I bring to the table that no one else can?* Your differences are your superpowers.

- **Your values:** What do you stand for? What problems—global, domestic, or at the community level—concern you? In which causes do you believe? To get inspired, have a look at the UN Global Issues or PwC reports. Climate change, equality, health, human rights, disruption, sustainability— these are just a few examples of causes that may drive your actions or give you a sense of purpose at work.

- **Your contributions.** Given your business experience or studies, what can you bring to the table in your industry? For example, perhaps you studied psychology and have insights into human behavior that allow you to offer valuable feedback to marketing teams. Maybe you're a user experience designer who understands how to create more accessible products. Or maybe your talent is analytics, and you know how to tell data-driven stories about why a business strategy is or isn't working. Whatever your area of expertise, how do you use it to add value to your individual work, team, or field at large?

The combined result of these three elements makes up your personal brand.

As an example, I'm a woman passionate about technology, with an international background, who has experienced the challenges of being a working mother and immigrating to a new country (uniqueness). I stand for equality and want to help people from diverse backgrounds find good jobs in our digital world (values). I lead a technical team at a tech company, and people come to me for career advice—tips around how to get into tech or how to upskill their workforce (expertise). Combined, these elements of my professional and personal identity create a personal brand that is entirely unique to me, my values, and my expertise.

What if you are not an expert yet? Don't worry: We are talking about building a *professional* personal brand, and that means all is possible in time and with learning. Even if you don't know or haven't developed the skills you need to be an "expert," you certainly have something to contribute. You just need to decide what it is, how much you can offer right now, and commit to developing yourself in that area. (It's also OK if this changes or evolves over time.)

Find Initiatives and Goals That Align with Your Brand

Now that you know the focus of your brand, you need to find ways to exercise it. Make it a part of your professional development goals. This way, it becomes a part of your regular workday.

Take a look at the projects your team is currently carrying out. Do any align with your personal brand? If so, raise your hand to participate. If you don't find what you're looking for, dig deeper and see what's happening at the organizational level. Big corporations often release annual reports around sustainability, DEI, workforce development, and other specialty areas. Read them and connect with teams working on the issues that pique your interest.

For example, is there an initiative that both aligns with your brand and that could use more support? I once worked for a huge telco and was eager to contribute to projects outside of my role. I discovered a team that was defining our organizational purpose, and while there were some permanent members, they were also seeking collaborators from other departments. I ended up leading a part of the project focused on building digital societies, which aligned well with my brand. I learned a lot, connected with people, and used it to share new insights with my manager and team.

If you work for a smaller company, be vocal about your skill set and ask how you can best support some of its public-facing projects. This is a great way to increase your visibility and showcase your brand both internally and outwardly. As I did, make sure you frame your participation as a developmental or stretch goal. It may even lead to your next big opportunity.

Connect with Colleagues Who Have Similar Interests

Making your brand a part of your work is an excellent start—but you can't go about it alone. You need colleagues with similar interests to inspire you, support you, shape your message, bring in new perspectives, and challenge your ideas so that you can refine them.

For instance, if you are interested in creating a more inclusive workplace for first-generation employees, and this is a key element of your brand, who can you connect with in the company to help you develop this goal, bounce ideas off of, and start building real community? Many organizations have employee resource groups focused on creating safe spaces for varying identities. That may be a good place to start.

Likewise, if your brand is more focused on an environmental, political, or human rights issue, look into whether your company may have existing discussion groups around these topics. You can also find like-minded employees by searching "your company name" + "social issue" online and seeing if any of your coworkers have posted on the topic—in an article or even on social media. Don't be shy around inviting people who inspire you to connect over a virtual coffee to learn more.

Finally, you can take the initiative yourself. Share articles or videos that you're passionate about with your team members or organize a "lunch and learn" on topics that align with your brand. This will allow like-minded people to come to you, help you expand your inner circle, and—who knows?—maybe even connect with new mentors or thought partners.

Create and Share Content

You're meeting new people and working on new initiatives. Now comes the essential part: creating and sharing content. Think of it this way: People move. Projects end or are killed. If this happens, you may end up like I did early in my career, starting from scratch. Sure, you can update your résumé and LinkedIn profile to reflect your work, but if you don't have content showcasing that work, no one will know what you actually did or what you stand for.

Block an hour or two at the very end of your day or week (or whenever is most convenient) to dedicate to content creation. An easy way to start is by reposting articles or news that align with your brand on social media channels like LinkedIn and Twitter. Don't just hit "Retweet," though. Add your perspective when you post. Over time, you'll grow more comfortable putting your thoughts into words, and may even be inspired to produce your own think pieces, social posts, or videos on those topics.

Creating original content will require more time and effort. But if your perspective is thoughtful, ethical, well researched (backed by evidence), and fresh, people will respond. Your personal brand will grow, slowly, but organically. Be prepared for people to provide you with feedback—positive, negative, and critical. Just as you're able to share your thoughts freely, others will share theirs. From this feedback, aim to learn, get inspired, reexamine your perspective or ideas, think of new angles, and create something stronger the next time.

Finally, as you reach people and gain more visibility, you can expect to get more opportunities to exercise your brand. This may look like being a speaker in your corporate all-hands meeting or delivering talks internally or at external event. With those invites, you'll be required to create new content as a part of your job, and you can use iterations of that work when developing new ideas to publish or post.

. . .

Remember: You are never "too busy" to work on your personal brand. Once you make it a part of your day-to-day job, it will come to you easily, and grow from there.

Adapted from "How to Build Your Personal Brand at Work" on Ascend, hbr.org, September 28, 2022.

6

You're Not an Imposter. You're Actually Pretty Amazing

by Kess Eruteya

D o you feel like a fraud? Many of us do. Perhaps you started a new job and believe you have less experience than you need, despite being the perfect candidate on paper. Or maybe your boss trusted you with an assignment that you feel totally unprepared to lead, regardless of your flawless track record.

There is a name for this feeling: *imposter syndrome.* Around one-third of young people suffer from it, and 70% of everyone else is likely to experience it at some point in their lives.[1]

Imposter syndrome is often tied to our identities and sense of self-worth. In the late 1970s, psychologists Pauline Rose Clance and Suzanne Imes coined the term in a research paper about high-achieving women, noting three critical attributes of the phenomenon:

- Thinking that people have an exaggerated view of your abilities

- The fear of being exposed as a fraud

- The continuous tendency to downplay your achievements[2]

Imposter syndrome typically shows up when we decide to take on new roles or new responsibilities, and it can result in feelings of self-doubt, anxiety, and guilt. Those who experience imposter syndrome may end up sabotaging their own success, obsessing over minor mistakes, or working twice as hard to prove themselves as a result.

If you are beginning a new (or first) job or just going through a change at work, overcoming imposter syndrome may feel impossible, like trying to remove a piece of clothing stuck to your skin. But if you fail to manage it now, it can have a detrimental impact on your performance and lead to burnout and depression in the longer term.[3]

Here are a few research-backed strategies that have helped me, and others, overcome these destructive feelings. You can become a better version of yourself at work, and in life, by giving them a try.

Keep a Positive Mindset

Many of us tend to downplay our achievements. In attempt to be humble, we brush them off by saying our success was just a product of "luck" or "good timing." While humility is admirable, too much of it can hurt rather than help you, especially if you are already fostering feelings of self-doubt.

Valerie Young is an expert who has built her career around studying and helping thousands of workers tackle imposter syndrome. Her doctoral research at the University of Massachusetts Amherst focused on observing and eliminating internal restrictions to success, with the majority of her subjects being women of color. While there are many systemic obstacles women of color face at work (and that we should not ignore), Young's strategy aims to empower individuals by encouraging them to intentionally acknowledge their accomplishments and abilities.

In a sense, this approach can be compared to mindfulness. When we push ourselves to remain in the present, as opposed to speculate about the future or worry about the past, we can focus more clearly on the reality of our situations and more easily let anxious thoughts go.

For example, say your boss has given you an assignment you feel you are not equipped to lead. Instead of ruminating about why your boss chose you or catastrophizing about all the things that could go wrong, stay present and acknowledge your reality: Your boss believes in you and trusts you to do good work.

Another tactic that I've found helpful is based on the advice of life coach and founder of Confident and Killing It, Tiwalola Ogunlesi, who recommends we acknowledge our achievements by completing a "monthly wins tracker" to chronicle our progress.

Essentially, you break a spreadsheet into two columns:

- Type of win (big or small)

- Descriptions (what actions you completed)

While completing the exercise, Ogunlesi emphasizes the importance of reflecting on questions that inspire you to discover your full powers. For instance, "What have I done that makes me feel capable?" or "If a younger me could see my life now, what would she be proud of?"

Ogunlesi's exercise was inspired by psychologist Martin Seligman's theory of well-being, which finds (among other things) that people feel more hopeful about the future when they look back on their life with a sense of achievement. "Imposter syndrome is just temporary memory loss, where you have forgotten all the amazing things about you," she told me. "We can mitigate imposter syndrome by reflecting on and reminding ourselves of our strengths on a regular basis."

Celebrate Your Wins

We often get so focused on the outcomes of our work that we forget to take a pause and honor ourselves. We worry that it is a waste of time or that it will make us seem like "show-offs." But celebrating yourself is a simple, and fun, way to combat imposter syndrome.

Ogunlesi suggests thinking about the many ways you can share the lessons you've learned from your accomplishments. "By reframing self-promotion as an exchange of value and self-enthusiasm, you can inspire others while mitigating your internal fears," she said.

For illustration, if you write a post on LinkedIn celebrating your new job, consider mentioning what you learned during the hiring process. Did you discover that you are resilient or the importance of soft skills? Whatever it was, don't keep it to yourself—you never know who you'll influence.

"There is no point being the world's best secret," Ogunlesi said. "You can have the best product or service, but nobody will know you exist if you do not put yourself out there." The more you put yourself out there, the more people will see you as a thought leader in your industry. While external validation can only go so far, seeing your brilliance appreciated by others can help you let go of the notion that you're a "fraud."

Finally, some of us need to more *actively* celebrate in order to feel the full force of our successes. If this sounds like you, consider taking yourself to dinner, texting a friend about your accomplishment, or even buying yourself something small. Whatever you choose, do something! It doesn't have to be huge, but it should matter to you. When we recognize our wins (regardless of their size), our brains release the feel-good neurotransmitter dopamine, which motivates us to accomplish even more.[4]

Make a Plan

This advice may seem obvious, but the idea here is to be strategic, not reactive. For instance, let's say you've tried the advice above and you still feel like a total imposter. What can you do? To avoid letting your nerves get the better of you, I would suggest coming up with an organized plan for success.

When you feel like a fraud, you may naturally panic. To prove yourself, you may produce a long list of goals and deadlines to hit without taking the time to strategize how you will reach them. As a result, you may end up entirely overwhelmed and unable to execute your objectives effectively. You set yourself up to fail before you even begin.

A better way to manage your anxious feelings is to get organized. Break down your goals into smaller, more manageable chunks and plan to tackle them one at a time. While completing a vast number of tasks can feel overwhelming, being consistent will get you far.

In his book, *Atomic Habits*, author and speaker James Clear emphasizes the impact of "one percent better every day." Set aside time on your calendar to work on your most important tasks of the week. I recommend scheduling a chunk of time for completing several smaller, lower-impact tasks (reading emails, copyediting, scheduling, etc.) and separate chunks of time to work exclusively on higher-impact projects (one by one). This way, you manage what you need to do in both the short and long term.

Last, you can protect your ego from the start by reminding yourself that you will face obstacles. In fact, you should expect and prepare for them to avoid any soul-crushing setbacks or surprises. Even the most accomplished people have room for improvement. Making mistakes is inevitable. If you learn from those mistakes, it's OK to fail every now and then.

· · ·

Part of the journey to overcoming imposter syndrome is learning from each experience you face. Not every piece of advice will work for everyone, so take notes along the way and reflect on what feels best to you in different situations. Adjust your plan based on your newfound knowledge, and keep adjusting. Imposter syndrome is a battle that you can and, with practice, will win.

Adapted from content posted on Ascend, hbr.org, January 3, 2022.

7

Advice for Early Career Professionals

A conversation with Paige Cohen

Early career professionals face a number of challenges, from navigating the workplace for the first time to figuring out what they want out of their careers. And for women, a double bind comes into play. How do you establish yourself and show confidence when others more senior are questioning you—to be seen as assertive but not aggressive? How do you advocate for what you want in those early years?

In this conversation, *Women at Work* podcast cohost Amy Bernstein talks with Paige Cohen, who oversees Ascend, a sub-brand under *Harvard Business Review* that offers work and life advice to young people worldwide. They answer questions that were submitted by early career listeners on how to speak up for themselves, their work, and the career they want.

PAIGE COHEN: Let's start off with a question written in response to a podcast episode of *Women at Work* called "Too Shy to Be a Leader." This person says she's actually pretty outgoing in life, but when it comes to work, she's shy, quiet, and more introverted. This is usually because she's questioning her own competency or the value of what she has to contribute at work.

Another recurring pattern she's noticed is that in performance reviews, she'll often get feedback that she needs to be more assertive. She wrote, "Granted, I'm sure there's always opportunity to be more assertive as a woman, but I'd like to think too much assertiveness could also be a point of criticism." She says that she wants to find a balance between assertiveness and persuasion. What are our thoughts on this?

AMY BERNSTEIN: This is the famous double bind that women face in the workplace and have faced since there have been women in the workplace. You have to be demanding but caring, authoritative yet participative. All of that stuff. Haven't you felt that?

PAIGE: Yes, definitely. I found this letter super relatable, even though I wouldn't say I'm an extroverted person. Especially in my first couple of jobs, I was very quiet at work, and I found it difficult to advocate for myself. And then when I did, I almost felt like I was being gaslit by my manager or by HR; I was being told I was bossy, or that I was just bothering people or being unreasonable. It was so hard to deal with, because as a young person in the workplace, I think everybody wants to be liked. So, if you feel like you're being bossy or annoying by asking for what you want, it's tempting to just shut down and be quiet. Is this something you've ever faced throughout your career?

AMY: Of course. But you've navigated this more recently than I have. How did you do it?

PAIGE: For me, it's been building up confidence by leaning on my strengths. I'm more of a quiet and shy person naturally. What I'll do, if there's a meeting I care about and I know I'll want to speak up, is practice what I want to say beforehand. This can seem tedious, but it's actually super helpful when you finally raise your hand to have rehearsed a little bit.

AMY: I 1,000% agree with that, and it is tedious. But when you're in that presentation and you know it cold, it gives you so much more confidence.

PAIGE: This idea of mixing assertiveness and persuasion is something I've had to navigate a lot, especially when it comes to winning over more senior employees. I've found that I've had to act "small" before I can act "big" around someone.

AMY: Say more about that.

PAIGE: When I first started working at HBR, I made this multimedia video. A person who was much more senior gave me this huge page of feedback. Some of it was good, but some of it was more about them asserting their authority: "This is my thing." So, before I could do what I wanted to do, I had to be overly verbal: "Thank you so much for this feedback. It's so important that you gave this to me, and I'm able to see it from all these perspectives now. This is going to help make the video so much better." I never had to deal with it from that person again, because they were like, "Oh, this person appreciates me, and this person trusts my feedback." That way I could start taking it in my own direction, and it was easier. That was a more persuasive way of being assertive than doing it outright, I would say.

AMY: Most people in that situation would have taken that really personally and might have even shut down after receiving a page of feedback. You read it for what it was. That's kind of amazing.

PAIGE: I come from a background of film school and creative writing, and in those situations, you're constantly getting feedback. Sometimes, people take your story personally. Sometimes people take your work personally. After a while, it just becomes emotionally trying to think too much about anything beyond "the work is the work."

If you're afraid to be assertive or if you're doubting yourself at work, it's helpful to draw those boundaries. It's empowering to say, "My work is my work." Something about that separation helps critical feedback become not as big of a deal. So, you go in, you do your thing, and you leave. If you don't overthink it, you might find that some of that questioning of your own competency or your value goes away if you're able to just have that boundary.

AMY: Let's take another question.

PAIGE: This one is from a 25-year-old woman. She works in the veterinary marketing industry. Her question is, "I am working on aligning myself to be in a C-suite position one day. Do you have any tips for how to set myself up for success?"

I'm curious what your first reaction is, Amy, given that you're kind of a badass boss at HBR and have been in so many leadership roles, and even VP roles, in the past.

AMY: The first thing I noticed about her is her ambition, and I salute her for it. Aim high. That is the only way to get to the top. The most fundamental thing I can say here is, don't lose sight of the job you're supposed to do, but look for every single opportunity you can find to demonstrate your ability to do additional work, your ambition, and your willingness to learn. It's the difference between coming across as a jerk and coming across as the teammate everyone wants to work with. You know what I mean?

PAIGE: Yeah, definitely. This question makes me think of an article that one of the *Women at Work* cohosts, Amy Gallo, wrote on hbr.org called "Act Like a Leader Before You Are One." You want to make your teammates and your boss look good.

AMY: One of the things that Amy says is, "Don't overstate your expertise. Don't exert authority where you don't have any. Use your influence to demonstrate your leadership chops." That is so important, and that's the thing about not being a jerk.

PAIGE: Yeah, I feel like at HBR, I've experienced this a little bit coming into a role. I came in as an associate, and I'm in a senior editor role now. A part of being able to grow—and this is another piece of Amy's advice and something that touches on my relationship with you—is networking and finding role models in people who are in positions that you admire and asking them how they got there and what you can do. It goes back to some of those conversations you and I have had throughout my years here.

AMY: Anna Ranieri, an executive coach, wrote an article for us that touches on that called "Convincing Your Boss to Make You a Manager." She points out that if you want to get somewhere, you have to figure out what skills you'll need. That's what a lot of the conversations between you and I have been about. You wanted to know what was required of the next step, and then you wanted to figure out how to both acquire those skills and demonstrate them. You seem to have a kind of intuitive sense about that. But it worked, right? Look where you are. It didn't take very long.

PAIGE: Yeah. I also applaud this person for their ambition, because I definitely was not at that place when I was 25 years old. I still don't want to be in the C-suite. It seems like way too much responsibility. But I think it's amazing that this person's already thinking about it.

Adapted from "We Answer Questions from Early Career Listeners" on Women at Work *(podcast), bonus episode, December 21, 2020.*

Keep Developing, Keep Growing

8

Make Continuous Learning a Part of Your Daily Routine

by Helen Tupper and Sarah Ellis

Our capacity for learning is becoming the currency we trade on in our careers. Where we once went to work to learn to do a job, now learning *is* the job. Adaptive and proactive learners are highly prized assets for organizations, and when we invest in our learning, we create long-term dividends for our career development.

Continual learning is important for everyone, regardless of career stage. But the risk for more experienced workers is that they get trapped in doing "more of the same," which reduces career resilience. To remain relevant and adaptable, those who have been working for longer need to prioritize making learning part of their everyday.

However, it's not as simple as acquiring new knowledge. In our increasingly "squiggly" careers, where people change roles more frequently and fluidly and develop in different directions, the ability to learn, unlearn, and relearn is vital for long-term success. Based on our experience designing and delivering career development training for over 50,000 people worldwide, working with organizations including Microsoft, Virgin, and Levi's, we've identified several techniques and tools to help you make learning part of your day-to-day development.

Learning

Since we spend so much of our time, energy, and efforts at our day jobs, they provide the most significant opportunities for learning. The challenge is that we don't invest intentionally in everyday development—we're so busy with tasks and getting the job done that there's no space left for anything else. Deprioritizing our development is a risky career strategy because it reduces our resilience and ability to respond to the changes happening around us. Here are three ways to take ownership of your learning at work.

Learn from others

The people you spend time with are a significant source of knowledge. Creating a diverse learning community will offer you new perspectives and reduce the risk that you'll end up in an echo chamber. Set a goal of having one *curiosity coffee* each month, virtually or in person, with someone you haven't met before. This could be someone in a different department who could help you view your organization through a new lens or someone in your profession at another company who could broaden your knowledge. You can extend your curiosity even further by ending each conversation with the question: "Who else do you think it would be useful for me to connect with?" Not only does this create the chance for new connections, but you might also benefit from a direct introduction.

Experiment

Experiments help you test, learn, and adapt along the way. There are endless ways you can experiment at work—for example, using different tools to increase the interactivity of your virtual and hybrid meetings, rearranging your meetings to increase engagement and productivity, or even trying out new negotiation tactics.

For an experiment to be effective, it needs to be a conscious choice and labeled as an opportunity for learning. Keep a *learn-fast log* where you track the experiments you're running and what you're learning along the way. It's important to remember that you should expect some experiments to fail, as that's the nature of exploring the unknown.

Create a collective curriculum

In a squiggly career, everyone's a learner and everyone's a teacher. As a team, consider how you can create a collective curriculum where you're learning from and with each other. We've seen organizations effectively use *skills swaps* where individuals share one skill they're happy to help other people learn. This could look like a creative problem-solver offering to share the processes and tools they find most helpful, or someone who has expertise in coding running beginner lunch-and-learn sessions. Skills swaps are a good example of democratized development where everyone has something to contribute and is learning continually.

Unlearning

Unlearning means letting go of the safe and familiar and replacing it with something new and unknown. Skills and behaviors that helped you get to where you are can actually hold you back from getting to where you want to be. For example, a leader might need to unlearn their default of always being the person who speaks first in meetings. Or a first-time manager might need to unlearn always saying "yes" as their workload increases.

Whether you're new to the workforce or have decades of experience, unlearning can feel uncomfortable. But we are all more adaptable than we give ourselves credit for. Here are three ways to make unlearning an active part of how you work.

Connect with challengers

We unlearn when we look at a problem or opportunity through a new lens. This is more likely to happen if we're spending time with people who challenge us and think differently than we do. The purpose of connecting with challengers is not to agree or debate but to listen and consider: What can I learn from this person?

Seek out people who have an *opposite experience* from you in some way. For example, if you're in a large organization, find someone who has only ever worked for themselves. If you have 25 years of experience, find someone just starting out. People who have made different choices and have different areas of expertise than you are a good place to discover a new source of challenge. Asking people, "How would you approach this challenge?" or "What has your experience of this situation been?" is a good way to explore an alternative point of view.

Identify habits and holdbacks

We all have habits that helped us get to where we are today. However, habits can create blind spots that stop us from seeing different ways of doing things or new approaches to try out. Our brains use habits to create mental short-cuts that might make us miss out on opportunities to re-flect on and unlearn our automatic responses.

Changing habits is hard, so to make progress identify *one habit holdback* that you have. This is something you do by default every week at work, and your hypothesis is that it's holding you back in some way—perhaps because it's time-consuming or you notice that your learning has stalled in an area. It could be a small habit, such as being the person who always sets the agenda for a meet-ing, or something more significant, such as being the one who solves other people's problems. Your job to do is to let go of that habit and try something new.

For instance, if you habitually jump to problem-solving, you could try asking open questions instead, like "What ideas do you have?" or "What have you tried so far?" Or if you're the person who sets a meeting agenda, ask for volunteers to take on that task for the next three months.

Ask propelling questions

Propelling questions reset our status quo and encourage us to explore different ways of doing things. They often start with: "How might we . . . ?" "How could I . . . ?" "What would happen if . . . ?" These questions are designed to pre-vent our existing knowledge from limiting our ability to imagine new possibilities. They fast-forward us into the future and prompt positive action in the present.

To put propelling questions into practice, it's helpful to pair up with someone else and take turns asking and answering questions. These five peer-to-peer propelling questions can get you started:

- Imagine it's 10 years in the future. What three significant changes have happened in your industry?

- How might you divide your role between you and a robot?

- Which of your strengths would be most useful if your organization doubled in size?

- How could you transfer your talents if your industry disappeared overnight?

- If you were rebuilding this business tomorrow, what would you do differently?

Relearning

Relearning is recognizing that how we apply our strengths is always changing and that our potential is always a work in progress. We need to regularly reassess our abilities and how they need to be adapted for our current context. For example, collaboration remains as important as ever, but maybe you're relearning how to do it in a hybrid world of work. Or maybe you've made a career change and you're relearning what it looks like to transfer your talents to a new setting.

Here are three ways to use relearning to stay nimble in the face of change.

Stretch your strengths

One of the ways to grow your strengths is to use them in as many different situations as possible. If you become too comfortable applying them in the same way, your development stalls. *Strengths solving* involves relearning how to use your strengths to offer support and solve problems outside of your day-to-day work. This could be in your networks, organizations you volunteer for, or even side projects you're involved in. For example, one of our workshop participants is a commercial marketing director who applies her creativity not only in her day job, but also through the successful brownie business she created during the pandemic.

Get fresh-eyed feedback

Looking at your skills from someone else's perspective will help you identify opportunities to relearn. Asking for feedback can help open your eyes to your development blind spots and take back control of your growth. When your objective is to relearn, we find that presenting people with *even-better questions* works particularly well to provide them with the safety to share candid feedback. For example: "How could I make my presentations even better?" "How could I make our team meetings even better?" "What's one way I could do an even better job of progressing my performance?"

Relearn resilience

Relearning takes resilience, and if you feel pessimistic about the progress you're making, you might be tempted to give up. Refocusing on what's working well can help you continue to move forward.

Try writing down three *very small successes* at the end of each day for two weeks. Your successes can come from your personal or professional life, and though it can be hard to spot them at first, the more you do this, the easier it gets. A very small success could include asking one person for feedback, helping a colleague prepare for a presentation, taking a lunch break, or cooking a new dish for the first time. At the end of two weeks, you'll have 42 very small successes, creating the motivation and momentum to continue investing in your development, even when it feels hard.

. . .

We can't predict how our careers will develop or what the world of work will look like in the future, but we can take steps to become more adaptable, no matter our career stage. Investing in our ability to learn, unlearn, and relearn helps us increase our readiness for the opportunities that change presents and our resilience to the inevitable challenges we'll experience along the way.

Adapted from "Make Learning a Part of Your Daily Routine" on hbr.org, November 4, 2021 (product #H06OF5).

9

Staying Up to Date in Your Field, Even as You Age

A conversation with Maureen Hoch

For the older worker, age bias often strikes when those around them assume that they're not up to speed on the latest technology or in the loop on what's hip or trendy for the youngest generation. They're written off as no longer an expert and feel overlooked and undervalued as their colleagues turn to younger coworkers for opportunities or answers.

In this conversation, Amy Bernstein and Amy Gallo sit down with Maureen Hoch, editor of hbr.org and supervising editor of the *Women at Work* podcast, to talk about how older women can stay curious and avoid being seen as out of touch—and when it's OK to admit you may not know something.

AMY GALLO: I want to talk about some the negatives of getting older at work: being invisible, being overlooked for things, being assumed you're out of touch. Does that ring true for you?

AMY BERNSTEIN: Totally. One thing you learn as you get older is that if you want something, you've got to ask for it.

AMY G.: That's good advice at any age. Why is it more important when you're older, though?

AMY B.: Because I think the opportunities don't tend to come your way as fast if you're an older woman. I'm sure it's true if you're an older man as well, but a lot of people assume that as their colleagues get older, that they don't want to continue to learn and grow. You have to communicate somehow that you want that opportunity to develop, you want to go to that conference—whatever it is. Asking for it is the way you communicate that.

AMY G.: But how do you make yourself visible? And maybe the answer isn't to be more visible, but to accept that people see you as invisible and you're still going to succeed. You're still going to do what you're going to do.

MAUREEN HOCH: You have to put effort into staying on top of your game. This is something that I think about in the context of working in digital media, where I have worked for many years. I worry about this a lot—that I've always been part of the "young web team" who are coming in to be the rabble-rousers and shake up the establishment. At what point do I become part of that establishment, or do I lose the air of someone who can manage that kind of work?

I really do believe that you have to put work into staying on top of that dilemma. We've written about spending time with people who are different from you. I like the idea of age as a form of cognitive diversity. Women especially make a mistake when they say, "Oh, well, that's for the young people; I can't possibly understand you young people." I don't accept that. There are ways for you to stay on top of what you're doing that will keep you current and keep you fresh. But they're not easy. You have to put effort into it. (See the sidebar, "Five Ways to Acquire New Skills—Without Going Back to School.")

AMY G.: How?

MAUREEN: I use many different strategies. Some of it is hiring people who bring some of that to the table. I use a very elaborate system of Twitter feeds and newsletters, and I also just talk to people. You have to be naturally interested in it, though. If all of that felt like work to me, it would be much harder to do. It's something that I'm passionate about and that helps a lot.

Five Ways to Acquire New Skills— Without Going Back to School

BY MARLO LYONS

- **Certifications:** Many careers offer certifications to prove you have a baseline understanding of what's required in a job or a mastery of best practices in a certain field. They are especially important if you're transitioning careers and don't have a lot of work experience in the new field.

- **Online learning courses:** There's a wealth of learning platforms out there, including LinkedIn Learning, Coursera, edX, Open Culture, and Khan Academy. While taking individual classes may not seem comparable to a four-year de-gree, showing you're continuously learning and growing your skills is an attractive quality in an employee.

- **Internships, rotations, and volunteering:** Most internships require that you be attending school to apply, but if you already have a full-time job, consider whether your boss would allow for a rotation in another area of the organization. Or seek training on your own time. For example, if you want to move into accounting, consider joining a school board or nonprofit board, vol-unteering at your child's school as treasurer, or setting up your own small company and taking on clients separate from your day job.

- **Stretch assignments:** If you have the bandwidth, ask for work from another department at your organization. You'll not only bring value to the company, you'll also enhance your visibility. Stretch assignments teach you new or higher-level skills while also challenging you to demonstrate those skills to the people who gave you the opportunity.

- **Mentorship:** The right mentor *outside* of your direct leadership or function will provide new perspectives on your work and how to uplevel your skills and challenge you to think differently. If you find a mentor who is a senior leader in your organization, they'll have deeper knowledge of the company's growth trajectory and what capabilities will be needed as the company grows or shifts strategy.

Adapted from "5 Ways to Acquire New Skills Without Going Back to School" on hbr.org, December 5, 2022 (product #H07DPD).

AMY B.: I'm not on the cutting edge of your young person's digital world, but one thing I do is when I hear a reference to something I don't know, I always write it down and look it up or I ask in the moment. I'm not ashamed of not knowing. I do think that once you give up on that—once you've lost your curiosity—the game's over.

MAUREEN: You have to stay curious. And you also have to believe in yourself, that this can be part of your world and that it's not somebody else's world. The benefit of experience is something that's hard for us to talk about sometimes. As a young person, maybe you roll your eyes at someone saying, "I have more experience at this than you do." But the fact is, that experience is what makes you so valuable as a mentor, to give advice, or to just help guide the people on your team.

AMY G.: I have a 12-year-old, and I'm trying to figure out how not to be the "cool mom" who's like, "Oh, I get TikTok, I watch it." I don't want to be that at work either. But sometimes I'll go to one of my younger colleagues and ask, "Can you please explain how Snapchat works? I don't get it."

How do you navigate that—acknowledging that you are somewhat out of touch yet not putting yourself in the corner of "I'm going to be dismissed," or "I'm so old"? Do you mention your age, your experience, or your maturity at work intentionally or do you leave it out?

MAUREEN: Amy B., I've heard you do this well in meetings when sometimes we'll be talking about something, and you'll say, "Let's not forget what's important here." You have a way of guiding people back to what's important.

AMY B.: That's my job, though, right?

AMY G.: But you also don't say, "In my X number of years in publishing, what I've found is important is . . ."

MAUREEN: You don't do that.

AMY B.: That kind of statement is always born of insecurity. I have never heard anyone say it in a way that didn't make me cringe.

MAUREEN: It's more being confident about what you know and what you're bringing to the discussion. You don't have to know all the ins and outs to be a good leader of that project, team, or what have you.

AMY B.: And it's just as important to know what you don't know, so that you can turn to someone and say, "OK, is this appropriate for Snapchat?"

MAUREEN: Exactly. And trusting those people. I mean, that is a situation where you just let those people run with it.

AMY G.: I'm sensing a theme here of just having confidence in your experience and confidence in your place in the organization or in life. There's no need to prove you have decades of experience. And there's also no need to prove that you know what "on fleek" means, although that's now many years old. But you don't have to prove it. You are just comfortable where you are.

AMY B.: I think you're right. There are enough insults that come with being a woman in your fifties that you have to grow a thicker skin. And you have to figure out a way to deal with the emotional challenge of disappearing, which does happen. You have to respond to it in a way that's constructive, that feels right to you, and that allows you to look at yourself in the mirror at the end of the day. And that cannot possibly include acting out of insecurity.

Adapted from "Aging Up, Not Out" on Women at Work *(podcast), season 4, episode 8, December 2, 2019.*

10

Why You Should Take on More Stretch Assignments

by Jahna Berry

You raised your hand for a stretch project, and—congratulations!—you've bagged the assignment. As an emerging leader, you were hoping to show your drive and ambition, but now that you have the opportunity, you're terrified.

They're called "stretch projects" for a reason: They require skills or knowledge beyond your current level of development and are great opportunities to shine in a new arena. This is also why they can feel so scary. Some people don't want to lead anything that they can't execute perfectly. But if you're willing to take the risk, and you do it well, you'll stand out.

Of course, the stakes are higher if you, like me, are queer, Black, a woman, or have other overlapping identities and work in an industry where you are a "first" or "one of the few." Botching an unfamiliar task is one of the most common fears I've heard during my decade as a mentor and coach to rising leaders of color and queer managers. Considerable research shows that women, people of color, and members of the queer community are punished more heavily when they make mistakes.[1] This is true at every level of experience, from CEOs to students. Those of us who share these identities know that a job setback or loss may be harder to recover from. It's no wonder we feel pressure to perform perfectly.

While systemic biases are real—and it's ultimately on leaders, lawmakers, voters, and industry watchdogs to tackle them—we are not powerless. There are things we can do to advance in our careers and get noticed right now. Based on my own career and experience mentoring others, I can tell you that, despite the initial fear, taking on a stretch assignment is usually worth it. Many of the promotions I've had can be traced back to saying "yes" to these opportunities. Handling unfamiliar work is a skill that you can learn and refine.

Here's how to tackle your next stretch assignment with unshakable confidence.

Recognize and Shift Your Negative Self-Talk

When you're starting a stretch project, it might be hard to not focus on everything that could go wrong. You may fear people will "find out" you don't know what you're doing or doubt your expertise or lean too heavily on the opinions of others. This is especially true for those of us who have overlapping identities or work in environments rife with microaggressions.

If you already feel pressure to perform perfectly, in a dark moment, you may experience thoughts like: "I don't belong here," "I can't do this," or "I'll mess this up." A key part of your success will depend on your ability to turn down the volume of the imposter in your head. (For more on imposter syndrome, flip back to chapter 6.)

Earlier in my career, I had the opportunity to lead the daily morning news meeting at a media outlet where I worked. My job was to steer news coverage, making sure everyone's voice was heard, asking smart questions, and keeping the dozen or so attendees engaged and productive. Until that point in my career, I had most often seen men or white women play this high-profile role. It was rarely, if ever, "owned" by a woman of color.

The first few weeks I led the meeting, my stomach was in knots every morning. Today, I recognize that my initial unease was a natural feeling. I was the only Black editor in the newsroom. This was often a theme in my career: I've been the only Black intern, Black editor, Black manager, and so on.

A good way to shift your mindset is journaling. This strategy has worked for many of the leaders I coach. When you're feeling overwhelmed by self-doubt, pause and take some time to reflect. Write down all the times that you tried something new and figured it out. It could be a skill you acquired at work that makes you proud, like public speaking, copywriting, or data analysis. It could also be something you learned outside of work, like a new language or how to make friends and build community in a new city.

Don't just jot down what you learned. Describe in detail any setbacks you faced, any fears you felt along the way, and how you overcame them. Reminding yourself of these wins will help you build confidence and give your mind the "evidence" it needs to prove that you're capable of taking on challenges.

Even now, as a chief operating officer, I sometimes use this practice in the face of new or challenging tasks that shake my confidence. Looking back at my journal entries helps me remember I can trust myself to eventually figure things out.

Get Clarity

Emerging BIPOC, female, and/or queer leaders working in predominantly white, male, heteronormative spaces are working in spaces that were not created with them in mind. This means you often have less access to stakeholders at the highest level of your organization than your white counterparts. You might also be less likely to have senior colleagues guiding and supporting you, especially early in your career.

If this is your situation, you may sometimes find yourself late to pick up on nonverbal cues or jargon that your peers know well—simply because you have not been in the room. For instance, you may not initially know that a C-level executive always twirls her pen when she wants you to wrap up a presentation. Or you may not know that people are sharing key information in Slack channels you haven't been invited to.

This guarding of knowledge can sometimes extend to the projects you take on, including stretch projects, which are more challenging by nature. At the start of your project, seek to gain clarity around your manager's expectations, important deadlines, specific goals you need to hit within those time frames, and any important stakeholders you need to keep in the loop along the way.

Schedule some one-on-one time with your manager to thoroughly discuss these points. During your meeting, ask how you should communicate your progress, who needs updates by when, and what medium you should use to deliver information. What decision points does your supervisor want to participate in? What team members, departments, or senior colleagues will the project impact? Most importantly, what does success look like?

For example, there may be a senior executive in another department who has unspoken or explicit authority over a part of your project. Once you know this, you can start to think strategically about their goals, and anticipate the questions they may ask you as the project progresses. You can even plan to meet with them to learn more about their expectations.

With every milestone you hit, check in with your manager or stakeholders about the original goals set, as many projects tend to evolve over time.

Do a Listening Tour

You may initially feel hesitant or nervous to meet one-on-one with senior colleagues or executives. A listening tour is a good way to overcome that fear, build bridges with the different teams, and fast-track the knowledge you need to execute this project.

At the start of the project, tell stakeholders and your manager that you plan to do a series of one-on-one meetings so you can get up to speed on the initiative. When you reach out, explain the project you're leading and what information you want to learn from them. Keep it short. You can say something like: "I'm reaching out because I'm spearheading X initiative. I'm talking to all the key stakeholders to learn as much as I can. You and your team are experts on X, and I'd love to touch base so I can learn more about how X works, how your team works, and how we can best collaborate."

Use your meeting to do three things: communicate transparently that you are not an expert in the area yet;

show a sincere interest in learning more; and give the people who are experts a chance to showcase what they know. Your goal isn't to immediately become an expert; it's to ask informed questions that will help you perform your role better. Try to ask similar questions in each meeting so that you can see patterns or other important information in your notes.

Here are a few questions that I like to ask during listening tours:

- How did you end up working here/on this project?

- What is your role and your team's role on this project?

- What should we stop doing? What should we keep doing?

- What is harder than it needs to be?

- How did we end up doing XYZ process this way?

- What are some things you're afraid I might get wrong?

- If you could wave a magic wand, what would you do?

- Who else should I talk to?

If the stakeholder shares their opinion but doesn't elaborate, follow up with something like, "Wow, that's an interesting observation. Why did you say that?" If they share a complex process that you find difficult to understand, explain that you're having a hard time digesting their point, and ask them to re-explain it as if they are talking to a relative who doesn't work in the industry. This will help them communicate more clearly.

While asking follow-up questions may feel embarrassing (especially if you are a younger professional and don't want people to doubt your abilities), the most important thing is that you understand how the pieces of your project fit together. Think of these conversations as an exciting opportunity to learn something new and to excel at your assignment. Don't let yourself fall into the trap of comparing your expertise to that of your coworkers.

When the conversation is over, thank the other person and ask, "If I come across something I don't understand, may I reach out to you again?"

People will appreciate your effort to educate yourself. No matter how senior they are, if this project and its success is important to them, they will want to support you and see you succeed.

Trust Your Gut

As you work your way through this exciting assignment, remember to cut yourself some slack along the way. Research shows that expertise is probably not what your new team or collaborators value the most. In Google's internal research on managing, subject matter expertise ranked *last* on the list of top eight qualities that make a good manager.[2] What mattered more? Excelling at the core task the manager was entrusted with—managing the team.

So, if you've been asked to project manage a big initiative, focus most of your energy on stewarding that project with excellence. (There's probably a good chance you were chosen to steer a project on an unfamiliar topic *because* you are a strong project manager.)

A major component of leading with confidence is trusting your ability to figure things out. That might be hard at first because, as a BIPOC, female, and/or queer aspiring leader, your personal sense of safety at work may come from avoiding criticism or constantly code switching. But remember, this project is an opportunity to hone new skills. Focus on learning how to sift through information, discern the most important details, and leverage *your own expertise* to make decisions. Don't let fear drive your decisions. Follow your intuition.

How do you distinguish the two?

I tell my mentees to use an exercise called "I knew better," adapted from the work of life coach Shirin Eskandani.[3] Write down all the times you had a hunch to do something but, against your better judgment, you didn't do it. In the end, if you found yourself saying, "I knew better"—that initial hunch was your intuition.

When thinking back to that initial instinct, what did that inner knowing feel like in your body? Remember this, and the next time you have the intuition to do something, write it down. Note when you follow through and don't follow through. The goal of this exercise is to use these moments as data points so you can learn what your gut instinct feels like when you're stuck at a pivot point during your new project.

. . .

Taking on a project outside your area of expertise is a terrific way to grow as a leader. Like any opportunity, it will put you in a situation where you need to navigate discomfort. Take the risk and raise your hand for stretch assignments that catch your eye. It might take your career in a positive, unexpected direction.

Adapted from content on hbr.org Ascend, April 7, 2023.

11

Learning Across Generational Divides

by Lynda Gratton and Andrew J. Scott

Coaching and mentoring across age groups makes sense. There is surely much each can learn from the other. We typically imagine that the young can help the old understand technology and the old can impart general wisdom.

But is there more insight into possible cross-generational learning than these commonplace observations? What else, specifically, can the young learn from the old, and vice versa?

To understand this issue, we designed a diagnostic and posted it on our website, encouraging people of all ages and from across the world to tell us about their work and life experiences. Over 10,000 people completed it. What we asked people was, at this point in their lives, are they actively building, maintaining, or depleting their tangible and intangible assets? Tangible assets include financial savings, while intangible included three important areas:

- **Productivity:** Valuable skills, supportive peers, good reputation

- **Vitality:** Health, managing work-life stress, and re-generative relationships

- **Transformational capacity:** Self-knowledge and investment in diverse and extended networks of friends and colleagues

Actively building both tangible and intangible assets is crucial to creating a long and productive working life.

Although we found that people of different ages are remarkably similar to each other, we did see a number of fascinating areas in which there were significant differences. Both the differences and the similarities enhance the possibility for bidirectional cross-generational mentoring and coaching.

What the Young Can Learn from the Old

How to control work

In general, we found that those over the age of 40 believe they are more able to control their work than those under 40. There is no doubt that for many people in their thirties, the demands of work can be tough: Some have young children to care for, bosses to impress, clients to serve. Faced with these many demands, they report having little control over the way they work, the hours they work, and their capacity to craft new ways of working. This puts stress on their families and vitality. It is no surprise that they say they are more exhausted than older workers.

Some older workers have learned how to exercise control over their work. They have learned what and when to delegate, when to push back on the demands of others, and when to accept demands. They have learned that some of the constraints they thought were immovable could be reframed by thinking more creatively about how they perform their tasks and what they consider the boundaries of these tasks.

It is these insights, honed over years of working, that could be of immense use to younger workers struggling to understand how to control their working lives. Working more closely in a coaching relationship would also sensitize older workers to the demands that their younger colleagues are facing.

How to be financially proficient

Learning how to build and maintain tangible assets is crucial to leading a long and productive life. Our calculations of savings rate and retirement planning make this clear. For example, if you live to 85 (which we believe to be a conservative estimate) and want to retire on 50% of your final income, then with an annual savings rate of 18%, you can plan to retire at 65; with an annual savings rate of 8%, your retirement age is 75. Having sufficient financial literacy to understand these choices and consequences is crucial.

Yet we found that in general, younger people are less comfortable with their financial literacy. Over time, financial literacy increases; in our sample, it was highest for people in their sixties. So it makes sense for the old to share their insights about finances with the young.

What might this look like? Financial proficiency has two key elements: financial literacy and understanding personal finances, and financial agency and control in terms of everyday behavior—particularly around self-control and placing a value on your future self. Both are crucial. Take savings rates, for example. Surveys show that most retirees wished they had saved more but did not have the self-control during their working life to save rather than spend. Older employees can help youngers individuals account for their future selves—by which we mean, understand that the decisions they take in the present will have implications on their future. As life and careers continue to lengthen, being better able to understand and support one's future self will become increasingly important.

What the Old Can Learn from the Young

How to build diverse networks

When we look at long, productive lives, it is clear that when it comes to intangible assets, the development of relationships and networks is crucial at any stage. The social capital embedded in these networks bolsters the acquisition of new skills through mentoring and coaching and can create the diversity of association which is so crucial to personal change and transformation.

We found that in general, those over the age of 50 are simply maintaining their current networks and failing to build new ones. As a result, their networks will become increasingly homogenous and static—simply too mellow and comfortable. This homogeneity will serve them badly if they want or need to transform.

It is second nature when people start their careers to reach out—to meet new people, build diverse networks, and actively find coaches and mentors. So why not encourage the young to coach the old in how to create and maintain diverse networks?

As personal life and working life expand, everyone will go through more changes and transitions. Having the skills and transformational assets to support this change tends to be something that is strongest in the young. However, as people live longer, they need to display this skill throughout their lives. Juvenescence, the art of aging young, is important, and this naturally opens up an avenue for inverse mentoring of the young by the old.

How to build a reputation

Interestingly, we found that being asked for advice was at its highest for those in their forties. Those over 50 reported that fewer people come to them for advice. Why might this be so? In part, it is because they are not making others aware of what it is they can bring—or perhaps are not themselves aware of the skills, knowledge, and wisdom they have accumulated. In a sense, they are not actively building their reputation. So why not encourage younger workers to coach older workers in what it takes to build a reputation and to attract others to them to be coached and mentored?

This makes all the more sense in a world where reputation is achieved not just through the linearity of a CV or conventional professional bodies but through the curation of social media. In this area, and in how to reach out and connect with more-diverse networks, younger employees can offer advice and insight.

· · ·

As working lives extend, different age groups will work more closely together. Creating opportunities for cross-age coaching could be a wonderful way to encourage people to understand each other more deeply and, perhaps, more compassionately.

Adapted from "What Younger Workers Can Learn from Older Workers, and Vice Versa" on hbr.org, November 18, 2016 (product #H039MZ).

Nurture Relationships and Create Support Systems

12

How to Make Friends Across Age Gaps at Work

by Jeff Tan

W hen I interviewed for my first job, I was focused solely on impressing the hiring managers. Getting an offer was the priority, and everything else came second. What I didn't think about was what life would be like after landing the role. It wasn't until much later that I realized how important the connections I'd formed with my coworkers had become. Not only did they provide me with community, but they also made me a better employee.

The next generation of workers appears to be a bit more in tune with what they want in a job (beyond the role and the salary) than I was in my early career. In a recent survey of more than 200 Gen Zers, participants reported that having a sense of community, along with paid time off and mental health days, is essential to them at work—something it took me several years to value.[1]

At the same time, new grads beginning their first jobs may find that a strong "community" is not so easy to form. The workforce now famously holds five generations, and if you're just entering it, you're likely joining a company with people much older than you are.

Some of your coworkers may be well established in their careers. Others may be at completely different stages of their lives—getting married, starting families, or buying their first homes. Suddenly, it may hit you: You're in a new environment. Not everyone is heading the same direction. Not everyone is invested in building relationships with their peers.

But don't be discouraged. There are incredible opportunities for professional friendship if you seek out the ones who are.

To successfully build relationships with coworkers of different ages, try a few of the methods that have worked for me throughout my career. You can apply them before deciding if an organization is right for you or use them to form deeper bonds with your colleagues after accepting a role.

Vet the Team Dynamic During the Interview Process

The first step to building strong relationships at work is ensuring that the company culture is designed to foster them. Asking the right questions during the interview process can reveal a lot.

To prepare, spend some time beforehand reflecting on the positive and negative learnings or work experiences you've had in the past. What kind of relationships did you value most? Will you be able to form them on your new team? Write down a few direct questions, and try to be as intentional and specific as possible.

When I decided to leave my first job as a life sciences strategy consultant, for example, I spent some time reflecting on what was and wasn't important to me at work. I took stock of all the relationships I had cultivated and discovered that I was willing to work much harder and much longer to support the people who I had the strongest connections with. I remember taking on an additional project and carving time out of my weekend to support a manager who had become more of a mentor to me. I didn't have to take on the project, but I wanted to support her. That, along with the extra experience and exposure, made it worth it.

Knowing this, I was able to seek out a similar experience in my next position by asking questions resembling the following:

- What's your leadership philosophy? or, What's most valuable to you as a manager?

- What kind of resources have you invested in to help cultivate a positive team dynamic?

- Do you (or does your boss) value relationship building across all age groups?

- Does your company have a mentorship program?

- In your opinion, how does forming strong connections with your coworkers impact performance?

Listen carefully to the responses. You can determine for yourself if their answers go beyond the generalities and really align with your needs. Do they realize the many benefits camaraderie has on team performance? Even if their answers are not perfect, you may see potential, and that's a good sign.

Create Opportunities to Connect

What if you've already accepted an offer? How can you start off on good footing with senior colleagues?

The first step is having the right mindset. It's easy to dismiss cross-generational relationships. After all, we come from different generations. We have experiences that may result in varied priorities, beliefs, and values.

Moreover, the more seasoned a colleague is, the more influence and power they likely hold. You may feel an added layer of pressure to appear knowledgeable or impressive when speaking with them. While this can be intimidating, don't limit your interactions to surface-level or transactional conversations. You might not realize it, but your older coworkers may be equally intimidated by you.

Try using the suggestions below to help you move past these feelings:

Think of your coworkers as peers

Viewing your coworkers as peers helps to shift your inner narrative and take away some of the pressure you may feel to impress them. When you change your perspective in this way, you may find it easier to be authentic and initiate more organic discussions. Though how you relate to each person will vary, I've personally found that sharing a sense of humor helps. That said, to avoid coming off too strong, begin by asking questions: How did they end up in their current role? What hobbies interest them? Simple conversation starters can help you identify common ground.

Set up regular one-on-ones

A monthly coffee or a virtual catch-up is a great way to get to know someone on a personal level. Just be careful not to overshare too soon. Sometimes we think that oversharing can help fast-track a connection, but in a work setting, it's usually better to let the level of comfort grow over time. After forming a foundation of trust, however, you can use these opportunities to exchange ideas, and even inspire one another. Once you both become more engaged, your relationship may become mutually beneficial at work (and beyond).

Listen diligently when they speak

The idea here is to remember the topics, interests, and values that are important to your colleague—just like you would with an important friend. This shows that you care about them and are genuinely invested. It's hard to remember all the details, so if you need to jot things down onto a notepad to remind yourself for future conversations, do it!

Know That Not Everyone Is Going to Be Your Friend

Try not to be disappointed if you don't naturally connect with someone you admire. Just like in life, you are going to connect with certain people better than others at work. You may end up building office friendships with a select few and have more professional working relationships with the rest. These aren't mutually exclusive, but it can be helpful to understand the difference.

Office friendships are usually rooted in shared personal interests and can nurture a sense of community and belonging at work. For instance, I became great friends with an administrative assistant in my last job. This person later became a mentor—not in a professional sense, but in a personal one. They passed down life lessons that continue to shape who I am today.

Working relationships are often rooted in shared professional interests and can help with your career development. An example that comes to mind is the strong working relationship I developed with a marketer at my former company. This person is a cancer survivor, and we connected over our passion to get our newest pharmaceutical drug to market. My mother was a cancer survivor as well, so we were both adamant about helping as many cancer patients as possible. Our relationship led to many professional opportunities that advanced my career.

Both types of relationships are valuable, and worth pursuing.

Ask for Advice and Invest in Developing Mentors

There are many senior employees who enjoy mentorship. For them, passing down the lessons they have learned throughout their careers is a reward in itself. Once you've comfortably settled into your new role and have made some connections, use the most meaningful ones to your benefit.

Think of your senior colleagues as resources who can help you solve the problems you are facing at work. Ask them how they would approach the situations you find challenging. Those who are enthusiastic to share their advice may have mentor, or perhaps sponsor, potential. A mentor or sponsor won't just help you develop professionally. You also need advocates in senior roles to build influence and social capital within your organization.

Currently, I work as the chief of staff at another biotech company. I'm one of the youngest members of our leadership team, and I sit with VPs who have much more industry experience than I do. To strengthen my relationships, I reach out to them whenever I want to talk through a new idea. I candidly ask for their feedback, not only on the idea itself but also on how I can best deliver it.

With each interaction, our connection strengthens. I learn more about the industry and how I can better inspire, influence, motivate, and lead those around me. Simultaneously, I gain the opportunity to show the VPs that I can be thoughtful and measured in my thinking, which in turn builds my credibility and their trust in me as a thought partner.

While you may not be on the leadership team yet, you can get there by beginning to foster these kinds of connections now.

. . .

Though taking these steps may feel overwhelming or intimidating initially, I urge you to stick with it. Sometimes, the challenge of forming a connection at work can become so big that we feel isolated and even consider leaving our jobs. In the end, you can't force a relationship. You are going to meet coworkers, especially older ones, who are not going to be as interested in connecting as you are. But there will also be people who are willing to make the effort, and those relationships can be life-changing. Pursue them.

Adapted from content posted on hbr.org Ascend, November 29, 2021.

13

Mentorship Goes Both Ways

by Cynthia J. Young

When I started my career as a sailor in the U.S. Navy, I knew I had to build a good rapport with my seniors to climb the ranks. The hierarchical nature of the job taught me that building strong relationships with my manager and more seasoned colleagues was critical to my growth and development. As I grew in my career, I also learned to guide those who enlisted after me. For a long time, that's all mentorship was to me—a linear relationship where seniors taught, supported, and advocated for their juniors.

A few years ago, however, my perspective changed. After retiring from service, I started my first stint in the corporate sector as a consultant. I was fortunate to have found a mentor in Bob, a senior colleague who helped me understand the culture, office politics, and emerging concepts in the business development space.

One week, we were working together on a new project that required us to research and understand an unfamiliar customer base. I suggested we try mind mapping, a visual method of organizing information. Bob was not familiar with the concept, but he didn't let that stop us. Instead, he asked me to walk him through it. His curiosity, enthusiasm, and willingness to accept what he didn't know—despite his seniority—taught me an important lesson.

That day I learned that mentorship is not a one-way street. Your age, experience, or expertise has nothing to do with the value you bring to the table. You have just as much to contribute as those who are seemingly more experienced than you.

There's a term for this—reverse mentoring.

The Case for Reverse Mentoring

Reverse mentoring describes a situation in which a younger or early career professional mentors a senior colleague. While the overarching goal mirrors that of a traditional mentorship—advancing the professional growth of the mentee—because the roles are reversed, this model shows everyone that experiential learning is just as valuable regardless of your age or expertise.

Junior employees gain more access to social networks and build their leadership skills. Senior employees gain a fresh perspective and expand their knowledge around new trends or technologies. Everyone becomes more engaged.

Further, when these relationships are built across departments, harmful silos are broken down and communication channels open. This, in turn, creates a competitive advantage for companies—strengthening their leadership teams, driving cultural change, and promoting diversity among teams.

If you're just starting out in your career and want to get involved in a reverse mentorship, here are five ways to go about it.

Figure out what you have to offer

Mentoring is most successful when you take the time to think about what you are qualified to teach, what other people in your organization may be interested in learning from you, and how it overlaps with your company's business objectives.

Before pursuing a reverse mentorship, think about:

- What lessons are you willing to share?

- What challenges is the company facing that you might have insights, information, or expertise on?

- How can you communicate your knowledge to someone else without overwhelming them or making it about yourself?

For example, let's say you are on the creative content team at a media outlet. Start by thinking about your business goals, how you contribute to them, and how you collaborate with other departments. Maybe you're in charge of the social media accounts and have expertise in copywriting, visual storytelling, and short-form video. You use these skills to help your company appeal to new audiences on different platforms. Now think about the other departments in your organization. How can your knowledge help them better do their jobs?

Perhaps you regularly collaborate with a senior colleague in marketing who has little knowledge around how you develop new ideas for your YouTube channel. Maybe there is someone in your finance department who provides you with a budget but knows little about your goals. What can you offer these people?

You can bring them value and help them do their jobs better by sharing your experience around how you think about your audience, how you develop content that you believe will engage them, the tools and processes you use, the challenges you face, the lessons you have learned around what works and what doesn't, and how you overcome obstacles. This will help the person in marketing better promote your content and succeed in their role. It will help the person in finance understand a completely new area of the organization and communicate better with your team.

The point is: Figure out what you're great at, why it is important to your organization, and how other employees (in your department or otherwise) could use that knowledge to grow as professionals.

Voice your desire

Now that you know what you have to offer, share your aspirations with your manager, colleagues, or peers.

Sticking with the previous example, during your next one-on-one meeting with your boss, you could say something like the following:

> *I have learned a great deal from the senior colleagues in our organization, and in return, I'd like to take the opportunity to share some of my skills within the organization.*
>
> *I believe that an opportunity like that would help all of us across different roles and hierarchies understand how we think, work, and make decisions. My unique expertise in content creation, I believe, would be especially valuable to some of the senior employees on our marketing team. It might also help us bridge generational gaps and be mutually beneficial in reaching our goals. I'd love to hear your thoughts on this idea.*

When it comes to sharing your idea with colleagues and peers, your best bet is to reach out to like-minded, curious individuals who may be interested in collaborating or taking you up on the offer. One easy way to go about this is to join an employee resource group (ERG)—that is, if your company has them.

Joining an ERG is a great way to meet and support people who you fundamentally connect to—regardless of age or expertise—and potentially find a senior colleague to build a mentorship with. It is a space specifically designed for listening, direct feedback, collaboration, and creative problem solving (at work and in life).

While formal reverse mentoring opportunities are usually set by the leadership team, you can also informally approach a colleague on your own. This often works best if you have already built a professional relationship with them. If you're working with a senior colleague from another department or reaching out to someone in your ERG, for instance, you can say:

> In the past two years, I've learned a lot from you. I was wondering if you'd be open to a reverse-mentoring opportunity where you can learn more about my work on the tech team and how we support the product team. My hope is that by reverse mentoring, we can both learn more about each other's skills, strengths, and priorities at work. What do you think?

Set clear expectations

Now you know what you have to offer and have expressed your interest. How do you actually begin a mentoring relationship?

This will depend largely on who you collaborate with. It might be a relationship that you have to work at and build up slowly over time—meeting casually with a potential mentee to discuss your ideas and areas of interest. It might end up being a more formal relationship—meeting regularly with a colleague who is ready to jump right in and learn.

Either way, make your intentions and expectations clear from the start. Together, you should discuss:

- **What's the objective of this mentorship?** Is it to help them build a new skill or to learn more about a different generation?

- **How will the mentoring be implemented?** Should it be a one-time activity, last a few weeks, or be a long-term commitment?

- **How will you measure your success?** Is there a goal they are aiming to reach? How often will check in on progress?

As your relationship grows, you should also make the effort to get to know your mentee beyond their work. The more you learn about each other, the easier it will be to open up and explore new ideas.

Be patient and humble

Recognize that reverse mentoring may be uncomfortable for some people, especially those in positions of power who are not used to being in the passenger's seat.

If you find a senior leader struggling to lean into their vulnerabilities, guide them with empathy. Ensure them that your conversations will be confidential and that you understand this might be hard for them. Reiterate that the goal of the mentorship is to learn from each other without judgment.

Essentially, model the behavior you want to see from your mentee. For instance, you could share with them a time when you similarly found it hard to adapt or to learn a new skill. Show humility by pointing out their strengths and admitting that there are times when you find it hard to master those very same things.

When you give people the time and space to be open, be themselves, and share their views—as opposed to growing frustrated or forcing change on them—you build a foundation of trust.

Likewise, don't rush your feedback or advice. It's not unusual for a senior mentee to feel sensitive to feedback or constructive criticism. There is an expectation that they should know more or "have it figured out" at this point in their careers, and they may feel pressure to live up to it. Helping them work through those feelings shows that you truly care. Give them the time to speak, share their thoughts, and ask questions.

Treat it like a continuous learning opportunity

Mentoring is always a two-way street, whether it is reverse mentorship or the traditional kind. While you're mentoring a senior colleague, use the opportunity to learn more about how things get done on their team, gain new perspectives on how decisions are made, and build your credibility as a young professional. Place them in your shoes by asking how they might handle the various challenges you face. Know that this isn't about showing off but a genuine intent on both ends to share what you have learned and benefit the other person.

Finally, remember that there's no right age to build a valuable relationship with a seasoned coworker. Reverse mentoring is a learning opportunity—always. As you grow into a more senior role, you will be able to share the feedback your mentee provided you with other junior professionals (and vice versa). That feedback will then be passed on and refined. It is a never-ending cycle, and one day, you will be the one looking up to those who come next.

Adapted from "Mentorship Is Not a One-Way Street" on hbr.org Ascend, December 1, 2021.

14

Build a Circle of Advisers

by Mimi Aboubaker

E veryone could benefit from having a kitchen cabinet of advisers, an informal group of people you trust, whose knowledge and perspectives you can call on when working through decisions to supercharge your professional (and personal) trajectory.

The term *mentor* is often anchored to this kind of relationship, but I find it limiting. For many, the "shoulds" and "shouldn'ts" attached to mentorship are stressful and can become a deterrent to pursuing much-needed support. Instead, I'd recommend swapping the term for *adviser*, and referring back to your high school days for a more approachable model.

In high school, students are often given the opportunity to develop informal advising or support relationships with a mix of people. You may have had this experience, too. These relationships typically form organically and can include academic advisers, athletic coaches, family, neighbors or community members, and even peers and near-peers. Together, these people make up a support network.

The professional world is similar. Your circle of advisers includes people with varying specialties. You have different levels of connection with each of them, and your relationships have the potential to strengthen over time. There are, however, a few important distinctions that can make finding advisers in your early career more challenging than it was in your teens:

- **Your priorities:** During your adolescence, classes, college, and fitting in were likely top of mind. As a professional, your priorities have probably shifted to career growth, finding the right job or organization, and fitting in culturally at your firm (e.g., interpersonal dynamics, office politics, and so on).

- **Your level of initiative:** For many of us, support networks were built into our high school or college experiences, especially if they included our family members, friends, or instructors. In the professional world, you have to proactively recruit supporters.

- **Your cadence:** Before, you may have had access to members of your support network weekly, or even daily. Once you enter the workforce, you need to be more intentional about when and why you reach out to people.

So, how can you find the right advisers for you?

A personal adviser scorecard is a framework I created that you might find useful. It outlines the most important factors you should consider when curating your circle of advisers and is meant to improve your understanding of yourself and your needs. Doing so can provide guardrails to the sometimes ambiguous networking process, and help you determine which relationships are worth pursuing and deepening.

My scorecard includes four categories that, in my experience, capture the most essential attributes you should consider in an adviser. Use figure 14-1 as a template when developing your unique scorecard and expand or adjust it based on your professional or personal needs:

- **Operating style:** Support type, engagement method, and communication style

- **Expertise:** Industry, skills, or knowledge possessed

- **Depth:** Long-term potential and capacity for deeper conversations

- **Extras:** Bonus categories based on your core values, interests, or support needs

Operating Style

Despite our instinct to group people based on jobs or backgrounds, we come in all shapes and sizes. When curating your advisers, it's important to tune into their

FIGURE 14-1

Personal adviser scorecard

Use the scorecard below to evaluate potential advisers and build a diverse circle of people who will meet your professional and personal needs. You can update each category based on your preferences and goals.

			Does the potential adviser meet your expectations or needs?			
			Exceeds	Above/ meets most	Meets	Below/ does not meet most	Does not meet
Operating style	Support type	Tactical	○	○	○	○	○
		Emotional	○	○	○	○	○
		Sponsorship	○	○	○	○	○
		Advice	○	○	○	○	○
	Engagement methods	Face-to-face	○	○	○	○	○
		Email	○	○	○	○	○
		Phone	○	○	○	○	○
		Text	○	○	○	○	○
		Casual	○	○	○	○	○
		Formal	○	○	○	○	○
	Communication style	Encouragement	○	○	○	○	○
		Radical candor	○	○	○	○	○
		Blend	○	○	○	○	○
Expertise	Domain expertise	Marketing	○	○	○	○	○
		Sales	○	○	○	○	○
		Finance	○	○	○	○	○
		Policy	○	○	○	○	○
		Financial services	○	○	○	○	○
		Technology	○	○	○	○	○
		Consumer goods	○	○	○	○	○
	Skills type	Soft: Self-awareness, communication, emotional intelligence, curiosity, etc.	○	○	○	○	○
		Hard: Financial modeling, coding, etc.	○	○	○	○	○
	Competency	Weaknesses: (list here)	○	○	○	○	○
		Strengths: (list here)	○	○	○	○	○
Depth	Familial	Socioeconomic upbringing	○	○	○	○	○
		Familial obligations	○	○	○	○	○
		Cultural affiliations	○	○	○	○	○
		Geographic roots	○	○	○	○	○
	Personal	Faith	○	○	○	○	○
		Sexual orientation	○	○	○	○	○
		Gender identity	○	○	○	○	○
		Other	○	○	○	○	○
Extras	Personal	Charitable giving	○	○	○	○	○
		Volunteering	○	○	○	○	○
		Civic engagement	○	○	○	○	○
	Professional	Firm affinity group	○	○	○	○	○
		Nonprofit board service	○	○	○	○	○

differences and how they match up with your preferences and needs, which will likely shift over time.

Operating style is one way to think about this—it can be broken down into three categories:

Support type

This covers the kind of support you need from potential advisers, and how capable they are of giving it to you. Though support comes in many forms, to keep things simple, you can categorize it as "emotional versus tactical" and "advice versus sponsorship." Our needs usually fall somewhere on the spectrum between the two.

If you're looking to ease your fears about a job application, for example, you need emotional support. If you're looking for guidance around how to prepare for a technical job interview, you need tactical support. If you're looking to be promoted or change industries, you may need a sponsor—someone to advocate for you when you're not in the room. In all these cases, you need advice (just different kinds). When you're building out your circle of advisers, consider who would perform best in these different roles to ensure all your bases are covered.

Generally speaking, I've found that near-peers are the most willing to offer tactical support, like résumé reviews and mock interview sessions. Mid-career professionals are more qualified to offer specialized advice around their expertise, and senior leaders are best suited to serve as sponsors or aid on big-picture career decisions and strategy.

Engagement

This is all about format, formality, and frequency. Does your potential adviser like to chat face-to-face, over email, by phone, or through messaging apps? How soon or far out do they prefer to schedule meetings? Is this person someone you want to share regular updates with, or is it someone you don't mind seeing biannually?

It takes time to feel out these preferences, but you don't need to formally ask people to be your adviser to accelerate the process. These relationships develop much like friendships. Whatever method you use, just be consistent about reaching out and maintaining the relationship. Their responsiveness is an indicator of their commitment.

Communication style

This is about what kind of feedback you find most effective, and whether the preferred communication style of your advisory candidates align with that.

Some people, for example, benefit more from words of encouragement while others prefer tough love. In my experience, it's best to have a healthy mix of people under this category. When you need a confidence boost, you'll want to connect with someone who fills you with pride; and when you need to hear the unvarnished truth, you'll want someone who can deliver radical candor. In the case of sponsorship, you'll want someone who's willing to guide and be honest about what you need to accomplish in order for them to feel comfortable putting their reputation on the line and advocating for your advancement.

As you shift and grow, bring new people with styles better suited to your current situation into your circle, and negotiate the terms of your existing relationships.

Expertise

Humans are mimetic by nature. We absorb behaviors and knowledge from those we spend time around. That's why building a circle of advisers who encourage you to stretch yourself is a simple way to accelerate your personal growth and expand your mindset.

Like operating style, expertise is multidimensional and can be broken down into three categories:

Domain expertise

This describes someone's knowledge of a specific or specialized field, and typically takes two forms: functional (e.g., marketing, sales, finance, etc.) or industry (e.g., technology, financial services, consumer products).

If you're still figuring out what career path you want to take, you could benefit from advisers who specialize in your functional area across different industries (e.g., financial services, strategic finance at a startup, and more). If you're looking to grow within a specific industry, a circle of advisers who each specialize in different areas of that industry (or who have different functional expertise within it) may be more beneficial, as you'll have a wide variety of subject matter experts to call upon as questions or challenges arise.

In either case, taking a holistic approach to building your circle will serve you for years to come.

Skill type

Skills can fall into two buckets—hard or soft. As an early career professional, you may be tempted to focus more on advisers who have hard skills that clearly align with your job responsibilities or interests (e.g., financial modeling, coding). But underdeveloping your soft skills (e.g., self-awareness, communication, emotional intelligence, curiosity) is a risk. As you move further along in your career, and particularly if you're interested in management, you'll spend a great portion of your time using those soft skills—which recruiters are finding increasingly desirable.

As you curate your advisers, be on the lookout for people whose talents are more intangible. These softer skills can look like someone who has strong verbal and/or written communication (e.g., a good storyteller, analytical writer, or structured communicator whose thoughts are easy to follow). These skills could also take the form of strong interpersonal dynamics (e.g., facilitates meetings in a way that brings everyone around the table into the conversation, capable of influencing others, has a magnetic personality).

Competency

Last, consider your strengths and development areas and seek out competent people in both categories. Capitalizing on your strengths will only benefit you, and people who share them—especially senior colleagues—can teach you how to practice them in useful ways. Communication, for example, is one of my strengths, and being around other people who value clear communication has helped me continue to learn, develop, and take pride in that skill.

In a similar vein, you can bolster your weaknesses by surrounding yourself with advisers who excel in those areas. A good adviser will teach you how to improve and actively nudge you toward a higher standard. If your company has determined certain competencies are essential to promotion, developing them is going to be critical to your growth.

Depth

"Bigger is better" is a narrative that most people are conditioned to believe, particularly early in their careers. But when it comes to your advisers, a smaller, highly curated group of people you can develop deep relationships with and who have the capacity to grow alongside you is typically better.

As you advance professionally, your career decisions will become more nuanced and include more personal factors—your partner's career, family planning, buying a home, your health, and so on. All these things can have a big impact on your choices. When you change industries, careers, or trajectories in general, your network will need to evolve with you. Choosing advisers who are invested in your long-term development will lower the churn rate.

So, how do you identify these people? I'd encourage you to consider all the dimensions of your identity and add the elements that are most important to you to your scorecard. The professional world has a tendency to be reductionist when it comes to this topic, throwing people into neat boxes labeled with gender, race, or institutional affiliations. Too often, we overlook the multiplicity of what shapes us and influences how we view the world.

Consider your socioeconomic upbringing, cultural affiliations, faith, sexual orientation, geographic roots, or any other factors that impact your person, and how they fit together to make you unique. Then, look for alignments in the people you meet or come across.

It can be helpful to review a potential adviser's published work, social media posts, or group memberships (on LinkedIn) to get a sense of whether your interests, dispositions, or identities align in meaningful ways. If you see things that resonate, they may be a good fit.

For example, if I were a student interested in technology and engaged with the foster care system, I might reach out to someone like Emi Nietfeld, a former Google and Facebook engineer who's written about her experiences with the foster care system and homelessness, as she could speak more intimately to my experience. Similarly, if I were undocumented, interested in finance, and unsure about navigating the compliance component of hiring, someone like Julissa Arce or Charlis Cueva, who have navigated those processes with Goldman Sachs, might be people with whom I'd able to form more intimate relationships.

The point is to look deeper than surface-level affinities and focus on the things that make people uniquely relatable to you. You can get personal guidance that is tailored to your needs if you make connections with this mindset early on. The more meaningful the relationship, the higher probability it has of enduring, as emotional resonance is an essential ingredient to strong relationships.

Extras: Bonus Categories

This is a free space to fill as you wish. For example, because living a life of purpose is integral to who I am, my bonus category is *purpose* (e.g., striving for impact beyond building generational wealth or making it to the C-suite). Purpose has manifested in different ways in different periods of my life—in middle school, I tutored students at no charge in classes; in the last few years, entrepreneurship has been my chosen vehicle for service, having built several mission-driven ventures. I see service as an integrated, lifelong practice and believe that philanthropy is a "give back" accessible at all ages and stages.

Your bonus categories should also be based on your core values, interests, or support needs. Some examples may be managing mental health, neurodivergency, caregiving, or work-life blend. Your values and needs have a strong influence on how you process career and life decisions. Having people in your network who see the world through a similar lens can be a powerful tool when making tough choices and planning ahead.

. . .

You've been building relationships your whole life. The professional realm isn't much different than the personal. You're still making connections—you're just talking about different topics. Building a cabinet of advisers is worth doing early in your career, as influencing and stakeholder buy-in will become more integral to success as you advance. Scorecards are a good exercise to ensure you are bringing the right people close.

Adapted from "Forget Mentors—You Should Build a Circle of Advisers" on hbr.org Ascend, June 29, 2022.

Navigating Challenging Situations

15

How to Say "No" to More Work

by Paige Cohen

H ow often have you heard the job advice: "Say 'yes' to everything"? The idea is that the more work you take on, the greater ambition you'll show, and the faster you'll move ahead in the organization. This wisdom was passed down to me through many generations—mentors, teachers, bosses, senior colleagues, and parents. Early in my career, I made them proud. I rarely, if ever, turned down a task.

I had an endless to-do list and spent late hours at the office paying my dues. Who cared if I was completely burned out and had no idea what I enjoyed or wanted to do? I was blessed with endless "opportunities." I was showing off great skills like organization and efficiency. I was a "yes" person—the best kind of person. What could be better than that?

Years later, I have the answer to that question: learning when to say "no." It took me a lot of trial and error to come to this, but gracefully turning people down has gotten me much farther than taking on non-promotable tasks for fear of disappointing others. Strategically saying "no" can afford you more energy, time, and work-life balance. It's a talent: the ability to prioritize work that will showcase your strengths or focus on tasks that will help you develop the skills you need to advance to the next level.

Like me, early in your career, you may feel more pressure to say "yes" to everything. It makes sense. You're new. You're trying to build a good reputation. Plus, as a woman, you're more likely to be asked to do non-promotable work—to take those notes or put in a quick lunch order. You may feel anxious about rocking the boat.

But remember: Reserving your energy for the most important work—the work that will benefit you and your ambitions—will make you more successful than taking on tasks you don't have the bandwidth to handle or would simply distract from bigger priorities.

Still, saying "no" is hard to do, especially if the requester is your boss. So, how do you do it?

I asked my team members, each of whom have a great deal of experience in this area, for advice.

Take a day to think about whether the task will help or hurt you

Saying "no" to my boss (or even my coworkers) is something I've always struggled with. I started my career in the startup world. As a member of a very small team, I learned the value of saying "yes" to every task thrown my way—even those that were far outside my job description. Not only did I learn a lot by doing so, but I also gained favor with my boss and earned promotions quickly as a result. I still carry this mentality with me even though I work at a much bigger company now.

I still think saying "yes" to tasks outside of your comfort zone can be really rewarding, but now I also understand the challenges that can come with doing so. If you say "yes" to everything, you're basically saying "no" to doing a good job at anything. There's a point at which spreading yourself too thin will cause a dip in your performance, and all that goodwill and experience you would have gained by trying something new goes out the window.

Now, when my boss asks me if I can take on a new task or project, I try to create a pause in the conversation by saying something like, "That sounds interesting! Would you mind if I get back to you tomorrow so I can look at my other priorities right now and see how much time I'd have to help out?"

From there, I think about the task itself and ask myself a few questions:

- Will I learn something new or gain experience by saying "yes"?

- Does this task align with my future career goals?

- What experiences will I lose out on if I say "yes" to this task?

- Am I already feeling overwhelmed?

These questions help me sort out if I'm actually interested in helping out with the project at hand, or if I'm just saying "yes" because I want to make my boss happy.

—*Kelsey Alpaio (she/her), senior associate editor, HBR Ascend*

Support your reasoning with data

Overloading yourself with tasks that you can't perform at your best will only lead to subpar results. When you say "no" to your boss, it's your job to make them understand that by using data and evidence to support your case.

The first step is to clearly understand the requirements of the task and estimate the efforts needed to complete it successfully. If you're unsure, ask your manager, "When would you need this done by and what would a successful result look like?"

Based on that data, consider your current bandwidth. If a successful result feels unrealistic, ask yourself why. One of the most common reasons may be that you simply have too much on your to-do list to take on the project in the given time frame. (If you have time, spend a day or two tracking how much time you're spending on each item on your current to-do list before answering your manager.)

Once you have a better idea of your bandwidth, find a time to speak to your manager one on one and calmly explain your situation, using any data you've gathered to support you. If the task is time sensitive or business critical and you can't turn around results fast enough, ask your manager to help you reprioritize the responsibilities you've already committed to. You can say, "I'd be happy to take this on, but I'm not able to get it done by the deadline given everything else on my plate. Can you help me reprioritize my to-do list to free up more space in my schedule?"

I've also found that collaboration tools like Trello and Airtable, which allow you to track your current tasks, can help keep you and your manager on the same page by making your workload visible to them. I recommend using these tools to document your pipeline of projects. Then share your pipeline with your manager so that they can see what you're working on before assigning you something new.

—*Dviwesh Mehta (he/him), regional director of South Asia and the Middle East, Higher Education, Harvard Business Publishing*

Don't just say "no"—explain why you're saying it

There's an uneven power dynamic when someone more senior than you, including your manager, asks you to take on a task. That's why it's important to outline the logic behind your answer, especially if you turn them down. Simply saying "no" leaves room for the requester to assume why you won't accept a task or are declining a project. Context is vital.

Examples of reasons you might say "no" include:

- You can't finish the task or project within the required time frame.

- You don't feel you have the resources to do the work successfully.

- You'll have to neglect important responsibilities to get the new task done.

In other words, if saying "no" will lead to a more efficient, balanced, and successful version of both you and your work, it's probably the right answer. As with most conversations at work, it's best to be transparent about what you notice, feel, and believe.

I suggest using phrases like, "I wouldn't feel comfortable doing this because . . . [state your reason]," or "With my current workload, I won't be able finish this task within the time you'll need." Sharing your logic with your boss will help frame you as a thoughtful, responsible, honest, and reasonable colleague.

—*Nicole Smith (she/her), editorial audience director,* Harvard Business Review

Adapted from "3 Ways to Say 'No' to Your Boss" on hbr.org Ascend, March 9, 2023.

16

Five Ways to Respond to Ageism in a Job Interview

by Rebecca Zucker

A s the global population ages, we will see increasing numbers of older employees in the workforce. Yet age discrimination is prevalent today. According to a recent AARP study, nearly two out of three workers age 45 and older say they have experienced age discrimination.[1]

Despite the negative stereotypes that older workers have less energy and are less productive, the data shows otherwise. According to research from the Stanford Center on Longevity, older workers are healthy, have a strong work ethic, are loyal to their employers, and are more likely to be satisfied with their jobs than their younger coworkers.[2] Moreover, a London Business School study showed that more people under 45 were exhausted (43%)

than those over 45 (35%), with the least exhausted group being those over 60.[3]

There are some jobs where gray hair (and the experience that comes with it) is viewed as an asset, such as C-level and more senior roles. Even then, an older candidate might be competing with a person—or be interviewed by someone—who is 10 to 20 years younger.

Sanjiv was in his late fifties when he interviewed as an internal candidate for the executive director role at a nonprofit. He knew the board was looking for a leader who could drive change, and he came to the interviews equipped with several new ideas for the organization. Nonetheless, he was told by the board member who interviewed him that they were looking for "younger minds."

Anita was laid off at the age of 55 after working at a large tech company for more than 30 years. Unemployed for nine months, she was starting to get discouraged after experiencing several incidents of ageism. One recruiter said outright that the company was looking for somebody younger, and a recruiter at a fraternity-like startup asked if she would have a problem with the late-night parties and drinking. She ultimately landed a great job at a large software company, where she was hired by a boss 20 years her junior.

Lauren was 49 when she interviewed and landed a job at a popular social media company, where the average age is under 30 and her boss, who hired her, was almost a decade younger than she was. Having interviewed with many big names in tech, she recognized that ageism could have been present, but says she hasn't felt it. Nonetheless, she was conscious of not sharing information that would allow others to "do the math" to determine her age. For example, while she was open about being a parent, when talking about her kids she intentionally did not share that they were in college.

If you are concerned about ageism, use these strategies to help make age a nonissue in your interviews:

Lead with energy instead of experience

Show your excitement about the opportunity and the work you do. Anita credits her success in her job search to her passion, which her boss still talks about. Instead of discussing how many years of experience you have, or how many times you've done a certain type of project, show your enthusiasm for the job by saying something like, "This is my sweet spot. This is the work I love to do." Calling out all your years of experience (no matter how valid or meaningful) can have the unintended consequence of alienating or intimidating your interviewer or making you appear to be a know-it-all.

Adopt a consulting mindset

Approach your interviews as consulting conversations, showing curiosity and a learning mindset. Use good open-ended questions, combined with engaged listening, to better understand the organization's context and unique challenges to identify where and how you can most add value. This approach will not only be more compelling but also will help you show up more confidently, as you elevate yourself to being a peer of your interviewer. The mindset shift is part of how you can change the perceived power dynamic from you really wanting or needing the job to you having the solution or know-how that the company needs.

Demonstrate humility and a nonhierarchical approach

Lauren attributes her success in her interviews to showing genuine humility and demonstrating an egalitarian approach in collaborating with others. She demonstrated this by asking questions like, "Where do you want to take advantage of the brilliant work the team has already done, and where do you think it might be time for a slightly different approach?" She also made a point to talk about "supporting teams" versus "running teams" and was sure to give credit to the people doing the work. Given that collaboration is generally the norm for Millennials, anything that signals a hierarchical style, like asking about title or span of control, is a red flag about one's ability to fit into a culture where the work is co-created.

Connect with your interviewer

Research shows that starting with warmth is an effective way to influence others.[4] This can be as simple as a smile. In finding ways to connect personally with her interviewer, Lauren made sure to use current references that a younger person could relate to, like a popular show on Netflix. Humor is another way to connect and show the other person you'd be enjoyable to work with. However, *do not* use dated references or self-deprecating humor like "that was pre-internet" or "that was probably before your time." It's uncomfortable and alienating.

Show your ability to work well with diverse groups of people

Anita illustrated this by giving examples of projects she led across multiple functions, geographies, and levels of leadership, including new managers. In doing so, she conveyed her ability to work well with younger colleagues, without needing to specifically highlight age. Similarly, Lauren conveyed that her intent was to take advantage of people's different experiences and gave examples of working well with people from the military who were having their first experience in the private sector. This example showed she could collaborate with younger people who had a different set of experiences without calling attention to age.

Reframe any inappropriate comments or questions

In Sanjiv's case, he could have reframed the board member's desire for "younger minds" by saying, "I think what you are really looking for is innovative thinking. I'd love to share some of my ideas that could help this organization amplify its impact and be a model for others in the field." When asked if she would be OK with the late-night parties and drinking, Anita kept it brief and said, "I love to celebrate success with my team," and then refocused the conversation elsewhere. If you're unsure how to respond to an inappropriate comment or question, respond with curiosity, asking something like, "Can you say more about that?" or "Can you share more about what you're hoping to learn, so I can address your underlying concern?"

While ageism exists, focusing on what you can control and employing these strategies can divert attention from your age and refocus it on why you are right for the job.

Adapted from content posted on hbr.org, August 2, 2019 (product #H052RB).

17

The Stigma Around Menopause Is Real

by Alicia A. Grandey

I n the United States, the average CEO is hired at the age of 54.[1] For many of us, middle age (40s–50s) promises to be the peak of our careers, in which decades of hard work finally pay off and we are seen as having the expertise, self-confidence, and stability necessary to move into high-level management and leadership roles. But for half the population, middle age also means another major shift: menopause.

The menopausal transition—that is, the period in which reproductive hormone levels become highly variable and menstruation cycles eventually cease— typically starts between the ages of 45 and 55 and lasts around seven years. During this time, women (or anyone with female anatomy) experience a range of symptoms, including both relatively hidden changes such as depression, sleep issues, and mood shifts, as well as the much more visible symptoms of hot flashes: unpredictable moments of overheating, flushing, and perspiration. And while the invisible symptoms are no less significant, many people are particularly embarrassed to experience hot flashes at work out of concern that being visibly "outed" as menopausal might harm their careers. But is this fear warranted?

To better understand the impact of hot flashes in the workplace, I conducted a series of studies (in collaboration with my colleagues Terri Frasca, Vanessa Burke, Didar Zeytun, and Jes Matsick) exploring the stereotypes associated with menopause, the potential costs to women's careers, and strategies to help men and women alike overcome these biases.[2]

Women Experiencing Menopause Seem Less Leader-Like . . .

In one study, we asked 300 U.S.-based full-time workers to share their first impressions of a hypothetical coworker who was described as "a menopausal woman," "a middle-aged woman," or "a middle-aged man." And in another study, we had nearly 200 college students read a workplace scenario involving a middle-aged woman described as having menopausal hot flash symptoms, a middle-aged woman without symptoms, or a middle-aged man.

In both experiments, the participants reported that the menopausal women seemed less confident and less emotionally stable (two traits associated with leadership) than the non-menopausal women—despite the scenarios being otherwise identical.

... Unless They Talk About Menopause Openly

The good news is, our studies also identified an effective strategy to overcome this bias. We asked more than 240 full-time workers to imagine that they were attending a meeting in which a female, middle-aged colleague was observed having a hot flash: She was visibly uncomfortable, flushing, fanning herself, and wiping sweat from her face. In one scenario, when a coworker asked how she was doing, she said, "I'm OK, just warm," while in the other scenario, she replied, "I'm OK, it's just that menopausal time of life." When the woman openly disclosed that her symptoms were caused by menopause, she was seen as more confident, stable, and leader-like than when she claimed to be "just warm."

We also determined that this effect held regardless of the woman's race or the gender makeup of the group: We tested scenarios in which the woman was explicitly described either as Black or white, as well as scenarios in which the meeting was either evenly split between men and women or male-dominated, and the participants consistently thought that the menopausal women were more leader-like if they openly disclosed that they were having a hot flash.

This may seem counterintuitive. After all, our first study showed that there are clear negative stereotypes associated with being menopausal. But our analysis suggests that the act of disclosing your own menopausal status conveys confidence and stability, essentially canceling out the negative biases that people would otherwise hold.

It's also important to note that it's not just that people appreciate getting an explanation for what's going on: In another scenario, participants were told to imagine that a *colleague* explained that the woman's symptoms were due to menopause, rather than the woman explaining the symptoms herself. These participants knew that the woman's symptoms were menopausal, but this knowledge didn't help as much as her sharing it herself. This suggests that simply educating people about what hot flashes look like isn't enough to overcome biases—to boost perceptions of leadership potential, self-disclosure is critical.

Normalizing Menopause at Work

Of course, while the benefits of talking openly about menopause and other workplace taboos are clear, many people are still understandably uncomfortable doing so. (See the sidebar, "What to Do When Menopause Is Taboo.") A recent survey of women in the United Kingdom found that almost half didn't feel comfortable disclosing their menopausal status at work, and in our own survey of nearly 100 women, about a third said they wouldn't talk about menopause at work, a third would share only with specific people, and just a third would disclose openly.[3] While some women felt that it was important to connect authentically with their colleagues about this "natural part of aging," those who felt less comfortable discussing menopause in the workplace expressed fears of discrimination and embarrassment.

Thus, to overcome bias against people experiencing menopause, it will be critical to build workplace cultures that encourage talking about it openly. Our research shows that especially for women who are actively striving to become leaders, acknowledging hot flashes when they happen and simply stating—without embarrassment or shame—that they are due to menopause is an effective way to demonstrate self-confidence and leadership potential. Moreover, each time someone talks openly about menopause, they normalize the experience and make it easier for others to follow suit.

At the same time, it's also important to recognize that it isn't the sole responsibility of people experiencing menopause to address these issues. Managers should strive to create psychologically safe workplaces in which everyone

What to Do When Menopause Is Taboo

BY MEGAN REITZ, MARINA BOLTON, AND KIRA EMSLIE

While the work of overcoming the taboos of menopause should *not* fall on women, the reality is that women going through menopause will confront uncomfortable situations with colleagues. If you are experiencing symptoms of menopause that are affecting your work, here are a couple things you can do:

Be Clear

If you are asked how you are or how you're feeling, if possible, give clear, plain responses and avoid euphemisms, which can confuse and perpetuate embarrassment. For example, at the start of a senior government meeting, one of us (Marina), experienced a hot flash and began to fan herself. A senior male leader in the meeting commented, "It looks like you're expecting a grilling!" Her heart pounding on the inside, Marina calmly responded, "Actually, no, I'm going through menopause, a symptom of which is extreme hot

feels safe to disclose issues and ask for support without fear of retribution or discrimination. To foster this type of workplace, leaders can start by being open about their own lives (whether with regard to menopause or other circumstances) and clearly demonstrating a willingness flashes." She further explained, "All women go through this experience, and we need to pay due regard to that in meetings such as these." The leader looked momentarily shocked but then became thoughtful. Marina appreciated his serious response: "That's a really good point, and clearly something I'm not properly paying attention to."

Speak Up, Together

If you aren't getting the support you need and you see something similar going on with other female colleagues, consider speaking up collectively. As we all saw with the #MeToo campaign, speaking up with a collective voice can have more impact. Within an organization, it can also feel safer to speak up as a group.

Menopause is one of the strongest, most impactful, and most discriminatory taboos still existing in the workplace. The mental and physical symptoms and their negative effects on productivity are needlessly exacerbated by poor policies and persistent, outdated gender- and age-related assumptions. We all can and should play a role in breaking the silence.

Adapted from "Is Menopause a Taboo in Your Organization?" on hbr.org, February 4, 2020 (product #H05EKH).

to listen to and learn from others' experiences. They can also help by supporting employee resource groups, providing educational resources to help everyone learn about the impact of menopause, offering accommodations such as cooler temperatures and fans, and most importantly, proactively challenging menopause stigma whenever it arises.

For half the global workforce, menopause is a natural (and unavoidable) part of life. It also happens to overlap exactly with the period in which people are most likely to be qualified to advance into top leadership positions. Thus, to avoid overlooking high-potential leaders in this important demographic, men and women alike must work to acknowledge and eliminate harmful stigmas related to menopause and the natural aging experience. It's up to those who have already made it to the top to build awareness, fight biases, and ensure that everyone feels supported—not silenced—as they progress through the phases of their careers and lives.

Adapted from "Research: Workplace Stigma Around Menopause Is Real" on hbr. org, December 20, 2022 (product #H07EES).

18

When You're Younger Than the People You Manage

by Jodi Glickman

More than 60% of Millennials and nearly half of Gen Z employees say they are people managers.[1] For some who are new to being a boss, adding the word *manager* to their title might feel intimidating.

Does that sound like you?

A manager is responsible for delegating tasks and assignments. While this will be one part of your role, the other part will be leading: bringing out the best in people and inspiring them to do great work, make sound decisions, and work toward a mutual goal. Among your first challenges will probably be managing and leading someone older than you. How do you engender their trust, respect, and admiration when there's a five- or maybe even a 10-year (or more) age difference?

Here are four key strategies you can put into practice:

Check Your Insecurities

A common fear of young managers and leaders is: My colleagues won't take me seriously. (Read more on this question in chapter 2.) You may find that this manifests in many different ways: "I look too young." "I sound too young." "Maybe I act too young." "How will my subordinates ever respect me?"

To get out of your head the next time you have these thoughts, try looking for real-world evidence that supports them. Then look for evidence that suggests the opposite. Ask yourself: "Would I have been promoted into this role if my supervisor, and the company, thought I was incompetent?" Probably not. You may find that your colleagues don't actually attribute competence or high performance to age. (And if they do, that's ageism, and you should probably tell HR or your manager.)

No matter what you find, remind yourself of this often: You belong in the seat you are occupying.

Get Everyone on the Same Page

People get picked to be managers because of their talents and people skills. This could be your ability to make sound decisions, bring different people together, influence others, and stay calm during tough moments.

When you start out, engage with your older direct reports in one-on-ones. Talk about your vision and goals for the team. Remember that they come with experience, and their experience can help you refine your ideas. Leave space for two-way dialogue and stay open to feedback.

Be Confident Enough to Be Vulnerable

If you are feeling unsure or insecure while leading, your team will be able to read that energy and may become unsure of your leadership too. That's why it's important to practice confidence when speaking to them: Make eye contact, use gestures to accentuate your point, stand up straight, and maintain strong body language. Practicing your delivery method will help you speak with conviction, be clear about your intentions, and show up as the leader you aspire to be.

At the same time, don't be afraid to be vulnerable and relate to your team during challenging projects or conversations. You're not expected to walk in day one and be an expert. You are, however, expected to be honest—about the obstacles your team is facing, the strategies you are contemplating, and your willingness to listen and learn from those around you.

When you share your ideas, leave room for your team to (honestly) reflect on them. Let them know that you value their opinions and experiences. You could say, "This is what I had in mind, and here's why. . . . What do you think? Do you agree? Disagree? Is there anything we're missing here? I'd love your thoughts and feedback."

Especially when it comes to older direct reports who may have been in the organization longer than you, solicit their opinions on what has worked in the past, what their current working style is, and where things are due for change. Ask how you can best support them. Say, "I know we started this new workflow last month. I wanted to know how you feel about it and take some time to review it."

When you do that, it's important to be receptive to their ideas and views. Be transparent about your desire to establish a true partnership. Your goal should be to bring out the best in one another.

Be Generous

Leaders who are generous—with their time, energy, and resources, with sharing credit and giving meaningful feedback—are the ones who earn respect and admiration from their teams. Generosity at its most basic is this: walking in every day and asking yourself, "How can I make my team's lives better or easier?" "What can I do to help them do their jobs successfully?" "How can I be an advocate for their ideas or support their initiatives?" "How can I showcase what they do right and have their back when things go wrong?"

Recognize that your older employees may be at a different life stage than you. Spend time to learn more about them, get a deeper sense of any barriers they may be facing, and how can you try to remove them—or at the very least, be creative in coming up with workarounds or ways to collaborate. For instance, you may find that one employee has to homeschool their kid during work hours. What can you do to support them and make their lives a little easier?

Being empathetic is critical to being a good leader. Do your best to accommodate different needs.

. . .

Great leaders of all ages show strength and humility, demonstrate a willingness to learn, and also show an ability to make decisions. Nothing about your age is a pre-determinant of your success as a leader. Rely on your transferable skills, build a solid team, and remember to set stereotypes aside as you venture into your new role as a leader.

Adapted from content posted on hbr.org Ascend, December 24, 2020.

It's Time to Fix the System

19

How Organizations Can Recognize—and End— Gendered Ageism

by Amy Diehl, Leanne M. Dzubinski, and Amber L. Stephenson

W hen a university vice president had an opening for a controller sitting just beneath her in the hierarchy, board members told her to seek an "older man" to complement her. Since she assumed the vice president role at age 37, board members had routinely criticized her age, calling her diminishing pet names like "kiddo" and "young lady." But being older wouldn't necessarily have made a difference, as another woman explained: "I am at the age when I should be getting the higher-level jobs; people in my profession now want to give the jobs to the 30- and younger 40-year-olds with the 'fresh, new ideas' as opposed to going with the person with experience."

Originally, ageism was understood to be prejudice, stereotypes, and discriminatory behavior targeted at older employees. Driven by the misperception that performance worsens and capacity decreases as people age, older employees are expected to just quietly leave so that younger talent can take the reins.[1] With an increasingly diverse and multigenerational workforce, age bias now occurs across the career life cycle.[2] "Youngism" refers to ageism toward younger adults and is fueled by the conflation of age with maturity and the misperception that tenure is required for competency.

However, research has only just begun to investigate how age is used to justify bias and discrimination specifically against women. Gendered ageism sits at the intersection of age and gender bias and is a double whammy where there is "no right age" for professional women.

In our recent open-ended survey research of 913 women leaders from four U.S. industries—higher education, faith-based nonprofits, law, and health care—we discovered that many women suffered from this "never-right" age bias. Conceptions of young, middle, and old age are often based on perceptions and vary between workplaces and contexts. When interpreting our results, we consider "young" to be under 40, middle age to be between 40 and 60, and older women to be over 60.

Gendered "Oldism"

As women age, they are often not seen as valuable or relevant in the way that male counterparts are. Older women in our research expressed that they were deemed unworthy of advancement. "While men become wells of wisdom as they age, older women are seen as outdated, harpy, strident," one physician noted. "Our voices are discounted." For example, a 61-year-old deputy chief information officer (CIO) was not considered in CIO succession planning. Instead, the current CIO was grooming a male colleague for the role. Another retirement-aged woman added, "I am largely ignored."

Many of these women felt discouraged, burned out, and resigned to not advancing any further. As a 66-year-old faith-based leader said, "At my age and with the mentality of our organization that they need men at the top, there is not a next professional step." Another woman in the same industry noted that once she turned 60, she was no longer "worth investing in with training or mentoring." Others felt compelled to find opportunities outside of their organization: "I am tired of proving myself to others and may as well do it in the interests of my own company," a 60-year-old lawyer indicated.

Gendered "Youngism"

Younger women—and those who looked young—were called pet names or even patted on the head, as one 39-year-old woman reported. Young women also experienced *role incredulity*, a form of gender bias where women are mistakenly assumed to be in a support or stereotypically female role. They reported being mistaken for students, interns, trainees, support staff, secretaries, paralegals, and court reporters. Such inaccurate assumptions were especially prevalent for non-white women, such as an Asian higher-education executive who appeared young and was presumed to be in a junior position.

Many younger women also experienced *credibility deficit*, which occurs when women's statements and expertise are not believed. "I am often told that I don't have the experience so I can't know what to do," one 34-year-old woman explained. In the face of such bias, women (and especially women of color) must expend extra effort to prove themselves. One young-looking Black university chief financial officer noted that she is often "pressed to provide a synopsis of her résumé to establish credibility."

Other younger women had their appearance scrutinized. One physician noted that between ages 20 and 40, men focused on her looks. After she gave a scientific presentation that she was very proud of, a male colleague told her that she "looked like a Barbie doll up there!"

Gendered "Middle-Ageism"

Unlike previous notions of a middle-aged "sweet spot," women between ages 40 and 60 in our study fared no better than their younger or older counterparts. One college leader described how some search committees chose not to hire women in their late forties because of "too much family responsibility and impending menopause." Other search committees declined to hire women in their fifties because they have "menopause-related issues and could be challenging to manage." And still other committees said that "women in their fifties and sixties may not have 'aged well' and do not 'look vital.'" Yet the jobs were given to similarly aged men.

A lawyer summed up the never-right age bias problem in her field:

> *First, we are too young to be responsible or to supervise. This lasts into our mid- to late-thirties but does not for men. (Perhaps they are waiting to make sure we don't have kids). Then in an instant, we are too old to be hired for anything or anywhere new. Once again, men are still "young enough" at the same age. . . . Women are young or old; we get no prime time even if we aren't out for childbearing or -rearing.*

In our research, we found that no age was the right age to be a woman leader. There was always an age-based excuse to not take women seriously, to discount their opinions, or to not hire or promote them. Each individual woman may believe she's just at the wrong age, but the data make the larger pattern clear. Any age can be stigmatized by supervisors and colleagues to claim that the woman is not valued or is not a fit for a leadership role.

Age diversity in the workplace yields better organizational performance while perceived age discrimination creates lower job satisfaction and engagement.[3] Similarly, gender diversity also matters. Organizations with diverse leadership teams perform better, especially in times of crisis; earn more; and have lower turnover.[4] The business case is clear—if organizational leaders pay attention.

How to Combat Gendered Ageism

The good news is that there are practical steps leaders can take to combat this never-right gendered age bias. Here's how:

Recognize age bias

You can't fix a problem you won't admit is there. Whereas sexism and racism are the focus of most workplace diversity, equity, and inclusion (DEI) initiatives, ageism has been largely neglected. All employees should be trained on gendered age bias, just as they are on other forms of discrimination. Use interactive case studies that include "gray areas" in age-related assumptions and address false stereotypes that older age reduces an individual's commitment, agility, and ability to learn. Company social media can also be leveraged to get the word out about ageism using messaging that taps into both emotions and facts. When the problem ceases to be ignored, necessary improvements can be made.

Address "lookism"

Much of gendered ageism is hinged on looks or appearance as a function of societal value. The incessant pressure to look young and attractive is something that typically impacts women more than men.[5] Include lookism in DEI training and ensure that it's not used as a hidden metric for hiring, promotion, or performance evaluation.

Focus on skills, no matter who has them

Younger women are often limited—whether intentionally or not—by the assumption of lack of experience. Middle-aged women may be thought of as difficult to manage or having too many family responsibilities. Women who are older are often constrained by perceptions that they are no longer invested in the organization, are less productive, or cannot be promoted. These falsehoods perpetuate the problem. Rather than focusing on age when hiring, making promotion decisions, or bringing on new team members for a growth opportunity, leaders should focus on each woman's skills, not their tenure or external demands.

Cultivate creative collaborations

Develop intergenerational, mixed-gender teams and professional relationships to encourage learning from each other and collaborating on solutions. Middle-aged and older employees have years of experience, while younger employees have perspectives from growing up in a more recent time. A recent study of Generation Z's expectations at work showed that one of their highest desires was for mentoring relationships; they long for connection with older workers who take an interest in them.[6] Too often women lack connections that would help them develop professionally due to exclusion from informal networks and events. Intentionally pairing younger women with older mentors and sponsors will aid their learning and career success and enhance your company's performance.

The research is clear: Any age can be viewed as "the wrong age" for a woman, allowing her capacity to be questioned and her fitness for leadership challenged. But we can stop stigmatizing women's age—benefiting not just women, but the whole organization.

Adapted from "Women in Leadership Face Ageism at Every Age" on hbr.org, June 16, 2023 (product #H07OJ2).

20

Six Ways to Move from Allyship to Activism

by Nahia Orduña

The business case for diversity, equity, and inclusion (DEI) is strong: Companies with a diverse workforce are 36% more likely to outperform their less diverse competitors.[1] That's why, in recent years, we've seen more businesses prioritizing DEI efforts—putting employee resource groups into place and publicly sharing their commitments to attract, support, and retain diverse talent.

But who is really behind these efforts?

Young women play a critical role in building diverse and inclusive teams, according to McKinsey's 2022 *Women in the Workplace* study—the largest of its kind in corporate America.[2] The study defines "young women" as those below the age of 40, and it states that this group is more likely to consist of women of color and women who identify as LGBTQ+. They're also more likely than both older employees and men in their age group to actively practice allyship at work.

As someone who has navigated the workforce for over 15 years as an immigrant, a tech leader, and a diversity advocate, this concerns me. Young women with intersecting identities are some of the most underrecognized employees in the workforce. While they're actively trying to push for change—whether or not it's a part of their job descriptions—their peers are focusing on tasks directly tied to promotions. If we actually want to move the needle and see these women move up into leadership roles, employees in positions of privilege need to play a much bigger part.

I'm not just talking about being an ally. I'm talking about being an *activist*. While many workers consider themselves allies, only a few *actually* take action. Activists, on the other hand, engage in the causes they support. We need both types of people to create an equitable workforce.

If you're part of the next generation of workers—the generation that's demanding diversity at work—you have the potential to drive real change. Allies, here's what you can do to step up into activist roles and contribute to the DEI efforts you want to see in place.

Learn the Difference Between Allyship and Activism

An *ally* is a person who supports diversity and wants to learn about communities outside of their own. In theory, a great ally asks insightful questions and finds ways support their underrecognized colleagues.

The problem is that "support" is a vague term. Liking or sharing a post on social media could be support. Wearing a pin in solidarity of a socially marginalized community could be support. But the data shows that too many of these gestures fall short. For instance, while three-quarters of white employees in the United States consider themselves allies to women of color at work, less than half of them are educated on the experiences of women of color or give women of color credit for their actions and ideas.[3] Only one in five white employees advocate for new opportunities for women of color, even though women of color say this is the single most important action an ally can take.

Activists, on the other hand, take action to promote their causes. They don't just educate themselves on an issue, they strategize what needs to happen to resolve it and work together to take steps toward that solution. Let's take a look at the feminist movement as an example. Activists organized demonstrations to raise awareness of women's political inequality. In the 20th century, they worked to influence policymakers, challenge unjust laws, and engage in political advocacy to challenge gender-based discrimination. They published literature and media and organized events to draw attention and raise awareness. At work, your activism may look different than it does in the streets—but it can be just as impactful.

Figure Out Where You Can Offer Value

If you're truly interested in shifting the burden of DEI work from the underrecognized person to the people, institutions, and systems that can initiate long-term change, evolve your ally mindset (*I'm here to help and support you*) into an activist mindset (*We're in this together*).

Think about your strengths. How can you offer people support in a way that either leverages your expertise or helps you learn something new? To answer this question, you'll need to first put on your ally hat. Educate yourself on the specific community you want to help and identify which of their projects, initiatives, or efforts needs more hands on deck. Then, start to take action.

For example, Neil, an activist I know, has a strong background in negotiating. He pitched himself to Women in Big Data (WiBD)—an organization that supports women in careers related to technology—and ended up joining their corporate giving workstream. Neil now uses his negotiating skills and experience to help WiBD secure donations from companies like Netflix and Databricks. Another activist in my circle has strong blogging and writing skills. He identified a gap in his company's DEI efforts—there was a lack of companywide communication—and created a corporate blog about diversity activities, giving voice to underrecognized employees.

Participate in Employee Resource Groups

If you're unsure where to start or can't think of a specific expertise to offer, you can get involved in the employee resource groups (ERGs) at your organization. I'm not just talking about showing up and listening (although this is important). I'm talking about lending an extra hand when the group needs it. ERGs often organize activities to help connect and build community among socially marginalized employees, which in turn can help those communities build stronger connections and aid in their career development. Activities might include inviting community leaders to speak, networking events, or casual get-togethers that focus on relationship-building.

One easy way to take action is to help organize these activities so that the community members can focus on the experience. You could help out with logistics or organize the event setup (virtual or in-person). There's always something to do—group members are usually doing this work on top of their daily jobs. In my own job, for instance, a few men regularly volunteer to help our women's resource group. One senior executive organizes our regular meetings, takes notes, distributes minutes, and uses his leadership, influence, and expertise around organizational politics to help us drive change. In fact, he led the creation of an early childcare program for our employees in Germany.

Actively Sponsor Your Coworkers

Sponsoring is different than mentoring, and you don't need to be a tenured employee to do it. Junior employees can make a huge impact, too.

Sponsorship happens when a person in a privileged position actively supports the growth of their less privileged coworkers by advocating for them or their work when they're not in the room. The sad truth is that some employees have more access to the big leaders and decision makers at their company simply because of their demographic background. This is a consequence of decades of bias, discrimination, and groupthink in educational and work institutions. While it's starting to change in some industries, it's changing slowly. If you're someone who is privileged enough to have access to the power players at work, you can be an activist by being a sponsor.

Start by paying attention and recognizing your own privilege. Ask yourself: "What doors have opened easily for me that have unfairly remained closed for my colleagues? How can I help change that?" You'll need to understand the work your colleagues are doing, and their larger career goals, to be a successful sponsor. This will allow you to drop their name when they're not included in a meeting or conversation. Use your access to promote their work, speak up for them, or tell management about their potential.

Another way to be a sponsor is to break down knowledge barriers. What tips and tricks have you learned from schmoozing with senior leaders at your company? How do you get their attention? What do they find valuable? In short, what are the unspoken rules to success at your organization? Give your colleagues feedback to help them navigate this terrain. This could look like encouraging them to take on stretch assignments or invite a senior leader to lunch. You can also give them guidance on the best way to address conflicts work, like how to escalate situations in a way that will get senior leadership's support.

Finally, know that you don't have to limit sponsorship to your organization. You can sponsor students by helping them land an internship at your organization or by connecting them to someone in your network who would be a good resource. You can even look into volunteering at youth organizations aimed at closing the opportunity gap for underrecognized communities.

Step in when You See a Microaggression

Microaggressions are insensitive actions, statements, questions, or assumptions that feel offensive to an aspect of someone's identity. Whether they are intentional or not, these biases can have devastating effects on the

185

mental and physical health of the people they impact—and most often, they impact socially marginalized communities. When microaggressions remain unaddressed or are repeated continuously over long periods of time, they can cause depression, stress, and burnout.[4]

For context, in the past year, half of 5,000 women surveyed across the globe for Deloitte's Women at Work study said they experienced microaggressions at work.[5] Ninety-three percent also said they believe reporting non-inclusive behaviors will negatively impact their careers. Women, of course, are just one of the many groups targeted by microaggressions, and if the majority feel unsafe speaking out, it's safe to assume that other marginalized communities share that sentiment.

As an activist, you can step up and help mitigate the problem, because it's not going anywhere until more of us do. When you witness a microaggression, don't be a bystander. Here are some common signs to watch out for and how you can respond:

- **Interruptions in meetings:** If you see that one person on your team is often interrupted, take the lead and call it out. You can say: "Maria didn't finish sharing her thoughts. Can we listen to what she has to say? I think it's very important that all our colleagues have a chance to share their ideas."

- **Discriminating humor:** Microaggressions can often show up in the form of slanders disguised as seemingly "harmless" jokes. If you notice this happening, speak up. For instance, if you hear a colleague share a homophobic or sexist stereotype in the form of a joke, you can say: "I know you didn't mean it, but that joke is hurtful to some people, and plays on a lot of harmful stereotypes. Let's be mindful of others."

- **Stereotypes:** If you see somebody making assumptions about a colleague based on their identity (origin, gender, age, sexuality, abilities, and so on), challenge their thinking. Educating yourself on what stereotypes can look like for various groups will help you respond thoughtfully. For instance, if you hear a sexist stereotype you can say: "I disagree that women are very emotional in the workplace. What are you basing that logic on? Most of the women I know react based on data, facts, and logic. There's research that debunked that stereotype a while ago."

Turn Your Actions into SMART Goals

As we've seen, there are many ways to be an activist at work. Whatever path (or paths) you choose to take, you'll make a greater impact if your end goal is specific, measurable, achievable, relevant, and time-bound goal, or SMART.

For example, let's say you decide to drive change through participating in an ERG. Breaking your goal down in this way will help you actually achieve it:

- **Specific:** I'll work with the women's resource group to plan and execute a companywide virtual event focused on educating employees on how to build a more equitable workplace. It will include a speaker with expertise in this area.

- **Measurable:** At the end of the event, I'll measure its impact by distributing a survey to participants, asking them how the event affected their understanding of diversity and inclusion (from 1 "no impact" to 5 "great impact"). I'll also track the number of attendees and collect quotes.

- **Achievable:** I'll work with the ERG to create internal marketing materials, identify speaker candidates, and run a technical check before the event. I'll use my organizational skills to moderate questions that people enter in the chat during the event. I'll also collaborate with other ERGs in the company to maximize participation and impact.

- **Relevant:** The purpose of this event relates to the company's mission of promoting diversity and inclusion. It will also help promote the ERG and demonstrate its value to the company.

- **Time-bound:** I'll plan and execute the event within the next six months and begin tracking feedback immediately after the event.

. . .

Truly equitable workplaces will arise only when everyone is willing to play their part. When we put the burden of work on the people being targeted by bias and discrimination, we fail them as leaders, as colleagues, and as peers. No matter where you sit in a company, you can participate. Don't just call yourself an ally. Use your position of privilege to push for change. Be an activist.

Adapted from content posted on hbr.org Ascend, May 16, 2023.

21

Three Strategies to Bridge Generational Divides at Work

by Heidi K. Gardner and Denise Roberson

In a recent conversation with the HR leader of a midwestern U.S.-based financial services company, she told us that older employees were confounded by the views and behaviors of Millennial and Gen Z employees, such as their insistence on working remotely, "fickle" work styles, and unbridled honesty when work wasn't going their way. Conversely, the younger set found the company veterans to be inflexible, uncreative, and often naive in their willingness to take company leaders' word at face value.

These differences were exacerbated by the organization's hierarchical culture, where senior employees—who were invariably older—had their own meetings, their own wings of the office, and their own client relationships.

And when intergenerational collaboration did take place, the more tenured colleagues dominated the conversation. The result? Disengaged younger workers, stagnant older workers, and poorer, less comprehensive solutions for clients. As much as senior executives touted the ability to attract next-generation workers as evidence of the company's growth and appeal, midlevel managers groaned at all the friction it created.

Generational disconnect is an ages-old problem. But for the first time ever, we have five generations in the workforce. And company leaders are balancing the call for more purposeful work from their employees with ever-increasing performance demands to succeed in their markets. Sometimes it seems that these two forces are diametrically opposed, causing leaders to favor performance over purpose or pay superficial attention to the company's proclaimed mission.

Based on our combined decades of academic and applied research as well as our hands-on experience inside and advising some of the world's most progressive companies, we've learned that bringing together different age cohorts fosters a shared sense of purpose in a company, as well as better business outcomes. Companies that capitalize on friction between generations and use it to spark creativity flourish by instilling a sense of purpose across their whole employee base, innovating faster, and forging stronger bonds with their customers.

The Problem and Promise of Age Diversity

Because it's so observable in the way people look and talk, age diversity makes people especially prone to "us versus them" thinking. It's human nature to trust and affiliate with people whom we perceive to be part of our in-group. Leaders need to actively foster a common identity and understanding across generations so that people are more likely to appreciate and include people of different ages. Investing in understanding others' different points of view creates common knowledge, which is the cornerstone of effective collaboration: It gives a group a frame of reference, allows them to interpret situations and decisions correctly, helps people understand one another better, and greatly increases efficiency.

Nevertheless, we also find that smart, well-intentioned people often fail to make the most of age diversity because they don't know how to strategically manage these differences. Leaders create project teams with people of diverse ages, invite everyone to holiday potlucks, and create common spaces where they'll ideally cross paths and brainstorm. But this laissez-faire approach doesn't work because the differences are more obvious than the benefits.

Here are three approaches that help people not only see the value in age differences, but also use that diversity to boost employee retention and productivity, innovate more consistently, and deepen customer relationships.

Build and Capitalize on a Shared Sense of Purpose

A survey by McKinsey underscored the renewed importance of purpose: Nearly two-thirds of U.S.-based employees said that Covid-19 had caused them to reflect on their purpose in life.[1] And Millennials were three times more likely than others to say they were reevaluating the type of work they do because of the pandemic. According to one senior executive at an educational software company we spoke with, "Our senior managers are repeatedly flabbergasted when a Millennial pushes back and says, 'Why should we spend time on this if it doesn't contribute to social justice?'"

In our work with global companies across industries, we've found that leaders who recognize and act intentionally to bridge this generational gap are much more likely to foster a more cohesive, energized workforce. Hold town hall meetings that put people in mixed-generation groups (of around six to eight people) and have them answer a set of questions about purpose together. Center the questions on linking one's personal purpose with the corporate purpose so employees can see how they and their work contribute to it. For example: "What is most important to you in your day-to-day life? How does this tie into your work at our company?"

What we've seen emerge from these facilitated sessions is that people have more similar values than they initially thought. More often than not, you'll hear responses like "family," "a sense of personal and professional growth," or "making the world a better place." This shifts into a conversation about how these priorities can be supported at work, helping people across generations feel heard and more engaged—a prerequisite to staying with the company and being a productive contributor. Highly meaningful work equates to a 69% reduction in an employee's likelihood to leave their company in the next six months and generates an additional $9,078 per worker per year.[2]

Use Team Launches to Highlight How Differences Matter

A shared sense of purpose among age groups unites and motivates. But differences among these cohorts should also be embraced and harnessed—for example, when a new team is just getting off the ground. The best teams have a mandatory kickoff meeting for every project, even if team members have already worked together. This way, they can get on the same page about each person's expertise, including the advantages they offer as a result of their age, tenure at the company, and life and professional experiences. For teams that don't do project-based work, leaders should find time to periodically hold "re-kick" meetings. Triggers might be the new budget season, an annual strategy review, or when new people join the team.

Have each team member create a scorecard at the start of a new project to outline their potential contributions based on their specific perspective. For example, Tina, a Baby Boomer, cites her decades of experience serving such-and-such clients, while Bernie, a Millennial, notes all the productivity software he's proficient in using. These scorecards form the foundation for the team kick-off meetings, ensuring that pertinent knowledge is unearthed and acknowledged. So instead of relying on who speaks loudest or most eloquently, members have a default reaction: "Who owns this this knowledge?"

To make sure age-related (and other) differences continue to be leveraged, we recommend that a director or senior manager assign the most trusted person (that is, the person most likely and able to have the best interests of all team members in mind) on the team to be the project's coordinator. Their responsibility is to understand each person's potential and see that it's brought to bear. This means comparing reality to expectations, and when there's a gap, figuring out why. Then, the fusion of contributions—by the right people at the right time, which we refer to as "smarter collaboration"—should spark innovation and customer delight. This leads to higher revenue and profit, deeper customer relationships, and a more profound sense of purpose and accomplishment among teammates. For example, one division of a tech company restructured its team approach with more intergenerational collaboration and had them create a team purpose. Post-implementation, they outperformed other divisions with higher team satisfaction and extremely satisfied clients.

Launch and Sustain a Reverse Mentoring Program

To forge even stronger ties between ages and generations, we recommend a reverse mentoring program. Reverse mentoring is when a more junior employee mentors someone more senior than they are. These programs can help senior executives or managers become more sophisticated about topics like social media, collaboration (younger people tend to work better on teams), work-life balance, and troubleshooting technology issues.

As the older group gains knowledge in these areas, they can develop a greater understanding of their younger counterparts' working styles and preferences. And they can become more self-reflective and open to change. For example, instead of wondering, "Why don't these people want to forge relationships with us in the office?" they might start to question, "Why don't I try to bring balance into my life by working from home when it makes sense?"

The mentor also benefits from a boost to their confidence and communication skills. There will inevitably be some give-and-take between them and their mentee, helping the mentor see their more tenured colleague in a more human and multidimensional light. With that said, it's important that this type of program be opt-in for both mentors and mentees and that the pairs are well matched based on what they're interested in teaching and learning.

Once the mentoring relationship is over (typically after six or 12 months), a human resources director or manager should assess what progress was made and how it can be leveraged to benefit the larger company. This evaluation is a huge opportunity to boost employee morale and further other top strategic outcomes. For example, it might spur a more intergenerational way of tackling client issues that leads to better solutions and relationships. Or it could serve as the basis for a kind of talent academy where each employee periodically teaches about an area of their expertise.

. . .

With five generations in today's workforce, age diversity is rich and brimming with opportunity. But these differences must be carefully managed—otherwise, perceived divides and barriers can lead to mistrust, contempt, and suboptimal solutions. Leaders can make the most of age and generational differences through fostering a shared sense of purpose in workshop sessions, using team launches as an opportunity to highlight differences, and setting up and sustaining a reverse mentoring program.

Adapted from content posted on hbr.org, December 23, 2022 (product #H07F5N).

22

I Was a Manager in an Ageist Workplace

by Nicole D. Smith

A few years back, I decided to chat with one of my team members, a man in his late fifties. I had recently started a new position as a manager—was just a few weeks on the job—and I wanted to see how people were adjusting to the change.

We found a quiet room and started discussing weekend plans and work projects. As the conversation continued, I found a moment to bring up something I'd been thinking about: "So I have an idea."

"OK," my employee replied, slightly suspicious yet curious. During my short time leading the team, I'd learned he was admired for both his talent and his tenure, so getting his buy-in could mean others would be open to my idea.

"I think we should get together with the digital team and learn more about what they do," I said. "They seem to be smart and innovative. I think they could really help our work and take us to the next level."

He was silent, which made me a little uncomfortable. But I pressed on, explaining what the collaboration could mean—like learning new tools and fostering the support of a creative, visible group.

But as I outlined my vision of partnering with coworkers who were mostly in their twenties, he was less than enthusiastic. In fact, for a moment I thought I saw worry in his eyes.

After what seemed like forever, he awkwardly shifted his body. "You're not going to force us to work with *them*, are you?" he asked.

This was the first of numerous concerning conversations I had over the next several days. I discovered that most of my team members—people in their fifties and sixties, many cherished contributors to our organization—had no desire to work with "those young people on the other side of the room."

I also learned I was in a culture that normalized ageist behavior—one where making surface-level assumptions about younger colleagues was acceptable. And it went both ways: Younger employees often disparaged older colleagues' supposed lack of technical skills and unwillingness to learn. They lamented, publicly and privately, that their knowledge, insight, and skills weren't appreciated and that they were being obstructed from developing and advancing.

After I required my team to work on projects with younger coworkers, they eventually began to collaborate with the digital team openly and often. But this was the first time I'd worked in an organization where people perceived each other's value, to some degree, in terms of their age rather than their contribution, commitment, and potential.

Combating Ageism at Work

Combating ageism all comes down to understanding. Lindsey Pollak, author of *The Remix: How to Lead and Succeed in the Multigenerational Workplace*, says managers can ignite change by creating multigenerational committees and seating arrangements: "What you tend to see in an office is all the executives of one age sit in one place, all the young people are in the bullpen, and all the middle managers are elsewhere. And I think that should be abolished." She also says managers must be deliberate in getting to know employees of all ages—and getting them to know one another.

Leaders don't have to let ageism quietly simmer, either. To spark change, start with language. Consider the comments, jokes, or labels people use to describe younger and older employees and whether they are microaggressions or are biased or insensitive. Overt terms such as *old-timer* and *youngster* should be eradicated, as should euphemisms like *seasoned* and *newbie*. Needless references to someone's age set the stage for conflict. Think, too, about what your work culture values. Studies show that organizations commonly use reward systems to shape norms.[1] In your company, are managers who hire up-and-comers as celebrated as those who recruit established stars? Do leaders equally laud the skills of digital natives and the institutional knowledge of older workers? Both are needed for an organization to thrive.

Younger workers (and hiring managers of all ages) should be encouraged to think about the assets that older workers bring to the table: experience, social skills, the ability to work independently. Similarly, older workers should understand what younger peers can offer, such as being tech savvy and valuing diversity.[2]

Finally, recruiting strategies should yield a diverse group of people, including older and younger candidates. Advertise with organizations that have members 55 and older as well as on job boards for college students and other relevant, frequently visited employment sites.

What I Learned

I still think about when I wanted to bring that group of older employees together with the younger digital team.

As a manager, I had to understand how ageist ideas were affecting our work—and then be brave enough to change the culture and create an environment where everyone, however young or old, felt comfortable. Knowing this problem wasn't something I could tackle on my own, I asked other managers to have their teams work on projects with my direct reports; to set a good example, we got in the trenches with them on those collaborations.

I also built a mixed-age team by hiring people over 60, under 30, and all ages in between; helping young and older workers see their ideas through and become more visible in the organization; offering training in new technologies to my team members; and promoting one of my oldest employees.

Despite the initial apprehension, my team and several others in the office eventually learned to work together without worrying about age. Through the years, we became more inclusive and creative. We challenged the status quo, and in some ways, we became the personification of the adage, "As iron sharpens iron, so one person sharpens another." Our differences helped us learn, and we made each other better.

Today, I challenge managers in my professional network to see the value in mixed-age teams. And I'm asking you to help all employees—from recent college graduates to those nearing retirement—see how pivotal their contributions are to your outcomes and organization.

Adapted from content posted on hbr.org, March 8, 2022 (product #H06WHG).

NOTES

Introduction

1. Lona Choi-Allum, *Age Discrimination Among Workers Age 50-Plus*, AARP Research, July 2022, https://doi.org/10.26419/res .00545.001.

2. Michelle Crouch, "Nearly 2 Out of 3 Women Age 50-Plus Regularly Face Discrimination," AARP, June 22, 2022, https://www.aarp .org/health/conditions-treatments/info-2022/women-discrimination -and-mental-health.html; "New AARP National Survey Reveals Close Link Between Discrimination and Women's Mental Health" press release, AARP, June 22, 2022, https://press.aarp.org/2022-6-22-New -AARP-National-Survey-Reveals-Close-Link-Between-Discrimination -Womens-Mental-Health.

Chapter 2

1. Rebecca Perron, "The Value of Experience: Age Discrimination Against Older Workers Persists," AARP, 2018, https://doi.org/10.26419 /res.00177.002; Peter Gosselin and Ariana Tobin, "Cutting 'Old Heads' at IBM," ProPublica, March 22, 2018, https://features.propublica.org /ibm/ibm-age-discrimination-american-workers/.

2. Christopher Bratt, Dominic Abrams, and Hannah J. Swift, "Supporting the Old but Neglecting the Young? The Two Faces of Ageism," *Developmental Psychology* 56, no. 5 (May 2020): 1029–1039.

Notes

Chapter 3

1. David P. Costanza et al., "Generational Differences in Work-Related Attitudes: A Meta-Analysis," *Journal of Business Psychology* 27 (2012): 375–394.

2. "The 'Kids These Days' Effect Is Actually Just an Illusion, Study Says," *Science Times*, October 19, 2019, https://www.sciencetimes.com/articles/24099/20191019/kids-these-days-effect-illusion.htm.

Chapter 6

1. Katie Garrett, "A Third of Millennials Suffering from 'Imposter Syndrome' in the Workplace," *Independent*, February 18, 2017, https://www.independent.co.uk/student/news/third-of-millennials-young-people-suffer-from-imposter-syndrome-in-the-workplace-confidence-mental-health-anxiety-jobs-careers-graduates-a7587066.html; Conor Murray, "What to Know About Imposter Syndrome: The Psychological Phenomenon Making People Doubt Their Success," *Forbes*, May 8, 2023, https://www.forbes.com/sites/conormurray/2023/05/08/what-to-know-about-imposter-syndrome-the-psychological-phenomenon-making-people-doubt-their-success/?sh=479c994460d2.

2. Pauline Rose Clance and Suzanne Ament Imes, "The Imposter Phenomenon in High Achieving Women: Dynamics and Therapeutic Intervention," *Psychotherapy: Theory, Research & Practice* 15, no. 3 (1978): 241–247.

3. Crystal Raypole, "You're Not a Fraud. Here's How to Recognize and Overcome Imposter Syndrome," Healthline, April 16, 2021, https://www.healthline.com/health/mental-health/imposter-syndrome.

4. Liz Guthridge, "Recently Succeed at Something? Celebrating Is Good for Your Brain," *Forbes*, June 24, 2019, https://www.forbes.com/sites/forbescoachescouncil/2019/06/24/recently-succeed-at-something-celebrating-is-good-for-your-brain/.

Chapter 10

1. Kenneth A. Couch and Robert Fairlie, "Last Hired, First Fired? Black-White Unemployment and the Business Cycle," *Demography* 47,

no. 1 (2010): 227–247; Katherine E. W. Himmelstein and Hannah Brückner, "Criminal-Justice and School Sanctions Against Nonheterosexual Youth: A National Longitudinal Study," *Pediatrics* 127, no. 1 (2011): 49–57.

2. Adam Bryant, "Google's Quest to Build a Better Boss," *New York Times*, March 12, 2011, https://www.nytimes.com/2011/03/13/business/13hire.html.

3. Shirin Eskandani, "The Key to Creating Your Best Life," ep. 138, in *Wholehearted Coaching*, podcast, MP3 audio, https://www.wholehearted-coaching.com/podcast/your-best-life-best-of-whc.

Chapter 12

1. Dawn Heiberg, "Gen Z in the Workplace: Everything You Need to Know," Firstup blog, October 18, 2021, https://firstup.io/blog/gen-z-in-the-workplace/.

Chapter 16

1. Kenneth Terrell, "Age Discrimination Common in Workplace, Survey Says," AARP, August 2, 2018, https://www.aarp.org/work/age-discrimination/common-at-work/.

2. Paul Irving, "When No One Retires," The Big Idea Series, hbr.org, November 7, 2018, https://hbr.org/2018/11/when-no-one-retires.

3. Lynda Gratton and Andrew Scott, "Our Assumptions About Old and Young Workers Are Wrong," hbr.org, November 14, 2016, https://hbr.org/2016/11/our-assumptions-about-old-and-young-workers-are-wrong.

4. Amy J.C. Cuddy and John Neffinger, "Connect Then Lead: How to Get Influence and Use It," hbr.org, August 21, 2013, https://hbr.org/webinar/2014/01/connect-then-lead-how-to-get-influence-and-use-it.

Chapter 17

1. "Average Age at Hire of CEOs and CFOs in the United States from 2005 to 2018," Statista, July 6, 2022, https://www.statista.com/statistics/1097551/average-age-at-hire-of-ceos-and-cfos-in-the-united-states/.

2. Rebecca MacGowan et al., "Untold Stories of Women at Work," *Academy of Management Proceedings* 2022, no. 1 (July 6, 2022), https://journals.aom.org/doi/abs/10.5465/AMBPP.2022.14525symposium.

3. Jamie Glasspool, "Report Shows Half of Women Are Afraid to Mention Menopause at Work—Female Leaders Must Speak Up," *IFA*, August 29, 2022, https://ifamagazine.com/article/report-shows-half-of-women-are-afraid-to-mention-menopause-at-work-female-leaders-must-speak-up/.

Chapter 18

1. "Millennials Are Managers Now," Zapier blog, March 10, 2020, https://zapier.com/blog/millennial-managers-report/.

Chapter 19

1. Sheila Callaham "Workplace Age Bias Hurts Early- and Late-Career Workers," *Forbes*, February 25, 2022, https://www.forbes.com/sites/sheilacallaham/2022/02/25/workplace-age-bias-hurts-earlyand-late-career-workers/.

2. Colin Duncan and Wendy Loretto, "Never the Right Age? Gender and Age-Based Discrimination in Employment," *Gender, Work, and Organization* 11, no.1 (January 2004): 95–115.

3. Yixuan Li et al. "Leveraging Age Diversity for Organizational Performance: An Intellectual Capital Perspective," *Journal of Applied Psychology* 106, no.1 (2021): 71–91; Jamie L. Macdonald and Sheri R. Levy, "Ageism in the Workplace: The Role of Psychosocial Factors in Predicting Job Satisfaction, Commitment, and Engagement," *Journal of Social Issues* 72, no.1 (March 2016): 169–190.

4. Guy D. Fernando, Shalini Sarin Jain, and Arindam Tripathy, "This Cloud Has a Silver Lining: Gender Diversity, Managerial Ability, and Firm Performance," *Journal of Business Research* 117 (September 2020): 484–496; Marcus Noland, Tyler Moran, and Barbara R. Kotschwar, "Is Gender Diversity Profitable? Evidence from a Global Survey" (Working Paper No. 16-3, Peterson Institute for

International Economics, February 2016), https://papers.ssrn.com /sol3/papers.cfm?abstract_id=2729348; Muhammad Ali, Isabel Metz, and Carol T. Kulik, "Retaining a Diverse Workforce: The Impact of Gender-Focused Human Resource Management," *Human Resource Management Journal* 25, no. 4 (November 2015): 580–599.

5. Christopher Warhurst and Dennis Nickson, "Lookism: Beauty Still Trumps Brains in Too Many Workplaces," The Conversation, October 16, 2020, https://theconversation.com/lookism-beauty-still -trumps-brains-in-too-many-workplaces-148278.

6. *Work/Life: Helping Gen Z Flourish and Find Balance*, Springtide Research Institute, https://www.springtideresearch.org/research/ work-life; Andrew Deichler, "Generation Z Seeks Guidance in the Workplace," SHRM, June 28, 2021, https://www.shrm.org/ resourcesandtools/hr-topics /organizational-and-employee-development/pages/generation-z-seeks -guidance-in-the-workplace.aspx.

Chapter 20

1. Sundiatu Dixon-Fyle et al., *Diversity Wins: How Inclusion Matters*, McKinsey & Company, May 19, 2020, https://www.mckinsey.com /featured-insights/diversity-and-inclusion/diversity-wins-how-inclusion -matters.

2. *Women in the Workplace 2022*, McKinsey & Company, https:// wiw-report.s3.amazonaws.com/Women_in_the_Workplace_2022 .pdf.

3. The Intersection, McKinsey & Company, September 9, 2021, https://www.mckinsey.com/~/media/mckinsey/email/intersection /2021/09/29/2021-09-29d.html.

4. Ella F. Washington, "Recognizing and Responding to Microaggressions at Work," hbr.org, May 10, 2022, https://hbr.org /2022/05/recognizing-and-responding-to-microaggressions-at-work.

5. *Women @ Work 2022: A Global Outlook*, Deloitte, 2022, https:// www.deloitte.com/content/dam/assets-shared/legacy/docs/deloitte -women-at-work-2022-a-global-outlook.pdf.

Notes

Chapter 21

1. Naina Dhingra et al., "Help Your Employees Find Purpose—or Watch Them Leave," McKinsey & Company, April 5, 2021, https://www.mckinsey.com/capabilities/people-and-organizational-performance/our-insights/help-your-employees-find-purpose-or-watch-them-leave.

2. Shawn Achor et al., "9 Out of 10 People Are Willing to Earn Less Money to Do More-Meaningful Work," hbr.org, November 6, 2018, https://hbr.org/2018/11/9-out-of-10-people-are-willing-to-earn-less-money-to-do-more-meaningful-work.

Chapter 22

1. Jeffrey Kerr and John W. Slocum, Jr., "Managing Corporate Culture Through Reward Systems," *Academy of Management Perspectives* 19, no. 4 (2005), https://journals.aom.org/doi/10.5465/ame.2005.19417915.

2. "Hiring and Retaining Young Employees: What Are the Advantages?" *HR News*, August 13, 2021, https://hrnews.co.uk/hiring-and-retaining-young-employees-what-are-the-advantages/.

INDEX

Discussion Guide

Since the *Women at Work* podcast first launched, we've heard from all over the world that it has inspired discussions and listening groups. We hope that this book does the same—that you'll want to share what you've learned with others. The questions in this discussion guide will help you talk about the challenges women face in the workplace and how we can work together to overcome them.

You don't need to have read the book from start to finish to participate. To get the most out of your discussion, think about the size of your group. A big group has the advantage of spreading ideas more widely—whether throughout your organization or among your friends and peers—but might lose some of the honesty and connection a small group would have. You may want to assign someone to lead the discussion to ensure that all participants are included, especially if some attendees are joining virtually. And it's a good idea to establish ground rules around privacy and confidentiality. *Women at Work* topics touch on difficult issues surrounding sexism and racism, so consider using trigger warnings.

Finally, think about what you want to accomplish in your discussion. Do you want to create a network of mutual support?

Hope to disrupt the status quo? Or are you simply looking for an empathetic ear? With your goals in mind, use the questions that follow to advance the conversation about women at work.

1. The book argues that women can experience ageism at any point in their career—regardless of age. Share a time when you've experienced or witnessed age bias at work or with a potential employer. How did you respond? How did others around you react? Have you learned anything from these experiences that would change the way you would respond to a similar scenario today?

2. In chapter 1, Nancy Morrow-Howell described her reactions when asked about her retirement plans. Have you been asked or hinted about when to retire? How did that make you feel? If you haven't been asked, how did Nancy's conversation change the way you think about retirement?

3. Describe some of the stereotypical thoughts you have or have heard about other generations. In what ways can we recognize and counteract our own age biases? What steps can we take to prevent ageist preconceptions from influencing our thoughts and actions?

4. What parts of your own experience or expertise can you fold into your unique personal brand or professional story? How can you use them in your work or when meeting someone for the first time?

5. Share an instance where you felt like an imposter. How did you act in the moment, and what helped you to overcome these feelings? What additional support could you get for situations like these in the future?

6. What professional development opportunities exist in your company? Are they offered to everyone? What more can you or your organization do to provide options for learning, growth, and skill building?

7. In her conversation in chapter 9, Maureen Hoch mentioned that you have to stay curious to keep learning in your field. What areas in your work are you curious about, and in what ways can you keep that interest alive in a quickly changing workplace?

8. Describe a time when you've partnered with someone older or younger than you on a project or learning opportunity. How did that dynamic work? What did you take away from that experience?

9. What workplace relationships are most valuable to you? Do they include people across different age groups? How can you build more of these relationships and work together to combat age bias in your team or organization?

10. Mimi Aboubaker suggests building a circle of advisers in chapter 14. Do you have a such a group to support you? If so, who is in it? If not, what skills would be valuable for people in your circle to have?

11. Describe a time when your credibility has been questioned—maybe in a job interview, after a presentation, or as a young manager. How did that make you feel, and how did you respond, if at all? After reading this book, how would that response change?

12. In chapter 20, Nahia Orduña explains the difference between allyship and activism. Share some moments when you've observed allies at work. What actions have they taken beyond simple allyship to become activists? How can you and your colleagues encourage more of these behaviors?

13. Does your organization acknowledge age bias or tension at work? What adjustments need to be made to support generational diversity in teams, create a more inclusive workplace culture, and bridge generational gaps? What can you and others around you do to ensure these actions are successful?

ABOUT THE CONTRIBUTORS

Amy Bernstein, *Women at Work* cohost, is the editor of *Harvard Business Review* and vice president and executive editorial director of Harvard Business Publishing. Follow her on X/Twitter @asbernstein2185.

Amy Gallo, *Women at Work* cohost, is a contributing editor at *Harvard Business Review* and the author of *Getting Along: How to Work with Anyone (Even Difficult People)* and the *HBR Guide to Dealing with Conflict* (Harvard Business Review Press, 2022 and 2017, respectively). She writes and speaks about workplace dynamics. Watch her TEDx talk on conflict and follow her on LinkedIn.

Mimi Aboubaker is an entrepreneur and writer. Most recently, she founded Perfect Strangers, the United States' largest coronavirus crisis response initiative, which delivered 3 million meals across the country in partnership with government agencies such as the City and County of San Francisco, City of Oakland, County of Marin, and more. Prior to Perfect Strangers, she founded an ed-tech venture and spent time at Goldman Sachs and Morgan Stanley. For more tips on leaning in on career and life, follow her on X/Twitter @Mimi_Aboubaker and check out her website at mimiaboubaker.com.

Jahna Berry is an award-winning journalist, media executive, and an expert on leadership, management, and nonprofits. She has written about leadership for *Harvard Business Review, Mother Jones,* and OpenNews. She is a leadership coach who's worked with executive leadership programs at the Institute for Nonprofit News and the Maynard Institute for Journalism Education. She was a featured speaker at events for the National Association of Gay and Lesbian Journalists, *Wired,* the Online News Association, and the News Product Alliance. She is the chief operating officer at *Mother Jones.*

Marina Bolton is a former director of Organisation Development, Design and Learning and a Menopause Champion for the UK Civil Service. Marina is researching compassion and what it means to embody compassion as a way of being. Follow her on X/Twitter @marina_bolton.

Dorie Clark is a marketing strategist and keynote speaker who teaches at Columbia Business School and has been named one of the Top 50 business thinkers in the world by Thinkers50. Her latest book is *The Long Game: How to*

Be a Long-Term Thinker in a Short-Term World (Harvard Business Review Press, 2021).

Paige Cohen (they/them) is a senior editor at HBR Ascend.

Amy Diehl is chief information officer at Wilson College and a gender equity researcher and speaker. She is coauthor of *Glass Walls: Shattering the Six Gender Bias Barriers Still Holding Women Back at Work*. Find her on LinkedIn @Amy-Diehl, follow her on X/Twitter @amydiehl, and visit her website at amy-diehl.com.

Leanne M. Dzubinski is professor of leadership and director of the Beeson Leadership Center at Asbury Theological Seminary. She is a prominent researcher on women in leadership and coauthor of *Glass Walls: Shattering the Six Gender Bias Barriers Still Holding Women Back at Work*.

Sarah Ellis is the cofounder of Amazing If, a company with an ambition to make squiggly careers better for everyone. Together with her business partner Helen Tupper, she is the author of *The Sunday Times* number-one bestsellers *The Squiggly Career* and *You Coach You*, and host of the *Squiggly Careers* podcast. Their TEDx talk, "The Best Career Path Isn't Always a Straight Line," has been watched by more than 1.5 Million people. Prior to Amazing If, Sarah's career included leadership roles at Barclays and Sainsbury's before she became managing director at creative agency Gravity Road. Sarah also has an MBA with distinction and is a qualified coach and mental health first aider.

Kira Emslie is a voice and body language specialist working with the NHS leadership academy and Mountview Academy of Theatre Arts. She is an Estill Certified Master Trainer and works as part of the team at www .speakinguplisteningup.com. She is currently researching voice and the effect of emotions and hormones at NHS IAPT. Follow her on X/Twitter @KiraEmslie.

Kess Eruteya is the founder of InclusionZ, which assists top corporations in engaging diverse and youthful (Gen Z) audiences. She is also a keynote speaker specializing in innovation, diversity and inclusion, and corporate social responsibility.

Heidi K. Gardner is a distinguished fellow at Harvard Law School and author of the bestselling book *Smarter Collaboration: A New Approach to Breaking Down Barriers and Transforming Work* (Harvard Business Review Press, 2023). She cofounded the consulting firm Gardner & Co., and is a trusted advisor to boards and executives worldwide.

Jodi Glickman is a keynote speaker and the CEO of leadership development firm Great on the Job. She is the author of *Great on the Job* and a contributor to the *HBR Guide to Smarter Networking.* Connect with her on LinkedIn.

Alicia A. Grandey is liberal arts professor of industrial-organizational psychology at The Pennsylvania State University. She publishes innovative research on emotions in customer service and workforce diversity and shares her knowledge in workshops with business leaders. As founder of the Healthy-Inclusive-Productive (H.I.P.) Workplace Initiative, she strives to ensure science informs and benefits business organizations.

Lynda Gratton is a professor of management practice at London Business School and the founder of HSM Advisory, the future-of-work research consultancy. Her most recent book is *Redesigning Work: How to Transform Your Organization and Make Hybrid Work for Everyone.*

Maureen Hoch is the editor of hbr.org and the managing director of digital content for Harvard Business Publishing.

Marlo Lyons is a certified career, executive, and team coach and the award-winning author of *Wanted—A New Career: The Definitive Playbook for Transitioning to a New Career or Finding Your Dream Job.* You can reach her at www.marlolyonscoaching.com.

Nancy Morrow-Howell is a professor at the Brown School at Washington University in St. Louis.

Nahia Orduña is an engineer holding an MBA and a technical leader at Amazon Web Services. She is the author of *Your Digital Reinvention.* Learn more about the future of work and find free tools to thrive in the digital world at nahiaorduna.com.

Megan Reitz is professor of leadership and dialogue at Hult International Business School. She speaks, researches, and consults to help organizations develop more open, mutual, and creative dialogue. She is the author of *Dialogue in Organizations* and coauthor of *Mind Time* and *Speak Up.* Follow her on X/Twitter @MeganReitz1.

Denise Roberson is the chief purpose officer at Omnicom's TBWA\Chiat\Day. She is a trusted C-suite leader, board member, professor, and speaker. Roberson leads some of the biggest brands in the world to actuate their business case for purpose, increasing their brand value and competitive advantage while creating an engine for growth and innovation.

Andrew J. Scott is professor of economics at London Business School, having previously held positions at Oxford University, London School of Economics, and Harvard University. His work focuses on longevity and ageing. He is currently on the advisory board of the UK's Office for Budget Responsibility and the Cabinet Office Honours Committee (Science and Technology), is cofounder of The Longevity Forum, and is a consulting scholar at Stanford University's Center on Longevity.

Nicole D. Smith is the editorial audience director at *Harvard Business Review.*

Amber L. Stephenson is an associate professor of management and director of health-care management programs in the David D. Reh School of Business at Clarkson University. Her research focuses on the health-care workforce, how professional identity influences attitudes and behaviors, and how women leaders experience gender bias.

Jeff Tan supports corporate development and portfolio strategy at Agenus, an immuno-oncology-focused biotech, and previously served as the chief of staff. Prior to that, Jeff helped lead strategic business insights and new product strategy at Epizyme, another small oncology biotech, and spent time working in management consulting focused on commercial strategy in the life sciences.

Helen Tupper is the cofounder and CEO of Amazing If, a company with an ambition to make squiggly careers better for everyone. Together with her business partner Sarah

Ellis, she is the author of *The Sunday Times* number-one bestsellers *The Squiggly Career* and *You Coach You*, and host of the *Squiggly Careers* podcast. Their TEDx talk, "The Best Career Path Isn't Always a Straight Line," has been watched by more than 1.5 million people. Prior to Amazing If, she held leadership roles at Microsoft, Virgin, and BP and was awarded the *Financial Times* and 30% Club's Women in Leadership Scholarship.

Emma Waldman is an associate editor at *Harvard Business Review.*

Cynthia J. Young is the founder/CEO of CJ Young Consulting, which uses knowledge management practices to help organizations identify and overcome challenges. She is the author of *The KnowledgeManagement Memory Jogger.* Connect with her on LinkedIn @drcindyyoung and watch her TEDx talk, "A Knowledge Mindset: What You Know Comes from Where You Sit."

Rebecca Zucker is an executive coach and a founding partner at Next Step Partners, a leadership development firm. Her clients have included Amazon, Clorox, Morrison Foerster, Norwest Venture Partners, The James Irvine Foundation, and high-growth technology companies like DocuSign and Dropbox. Follow her on X/Twitter @rszucker.

ABOUT THE PODCAST

Women face gender discrimination throughout our careers. It doesn't have to derail our ambitions—but how do we prepare to deal with it? There's no workplace orientation session about narrowing the wage gap, standing up to interrupting male colleagues, or taking on many other issues we encounter at work. So HBR staffers Amy Bernstein and Amy Gallo are untangling some of the knottiest problems. They interview experts on gender, tell stories about their own experiences, and give lots of practical advice to help you succeed in spite of the obstacles.

Listen and subscribe:

Apple Podcasts, Google Podcasts, Spotify, RSS

Inspiring conversations, advancing together

 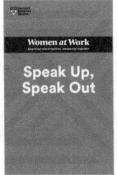 

Based on the HBR podcast of the same name, **HBR's Women at Work series** spotlights the real challenges and opportunities women face throughout their careers—and provides inspiration and advice on today's most important workplace topics.